Lost Houses of Newcastle and North

THOMAS FAULKNER AND PHOEBE LOWI

Foreword by Sir Roy Strong

The demolition of Low Gosforth House (Northumberland County Record Office)

JILL RAINES
1996

This publication has been kindly sponsored by Tennants Auctioneers

ISBN 0 9516494 2 6

Published by Jill Raines, The Grange, Welburn, York, YO6 7EQ
Telephone 01653 618590

Front Cover: Heaton Hall, Newcastle
Frontispiece: The Demolition of Low Gosforth House
(Northumberland County Record Office)
Back Cover: Haggerston Castle, Northumberland, Great Hall
(RCHME © Crown copyright)

Printed by Clifford Ward & Co. (Bridlington) Ltd.

In the same series
Lost Houses of East Yorkshire — David Neave and Edward Waterson
Lost Houses of York and the North Riding — Edward Waterson and
Peter Meadows
Lost Houses of County Durham — Peter Meadows and Edward
Waterson
Lost Houses of the West Riding — Edward Waterson and Peter
Meadows (forthcoming)

FOREWORD

by

Sir Roy Strong, Hon.D.Litt., Ph.D., F.S.A.

The exhibition *The Destruction of the Country House* staged at the Victoria & Albert Museum in the autumn of 1974 is recognised over twenty years on as a landmark in our awareness of the country house heritage. One of the reasons which made me aspire to be the Director of the V & A at the tender age of thirty-eight was that I was acutely aware of the crisis threatening the heritage in the early seventies. The new inheritance taxes and the proposed introduction of a wealth tax by the Socialist government posed a very real danger.

It was John Harris who came to me with the idea that we should do an exhibition on the topic, one which would put much of John Cornforth's important report of 1973 for the Historic House Owners into a form comprehensible by the general public. Arriving at the V & A on 1st January 1974 in the midst of the three day week and the fall of the Heath Government I pushed this exhibition into the existing schedule in the face of what was to become the usual opposition from the curatorial staff. The team which carried it through was made up of John Harris, Marcus Binney and Peter Thornton of the museum. By the time that it was staged a Socialist government was back in power and it was a courageous act to stage such a polemical exhibition opposing intended government policy, particularly when mounted in an institution which was actually part of government.

The idea of the polemical exhibition was in itself an innovation. That we were able to do it owed a debt not only to the begetters but to the fact that a director then had no need to fund-raise. He could utilise his budget for what exhibition programme he thought fit. Such an exhibition would today, in an age when every show depends on private sponsorship, never even get off the ground. Its impact at the time was enormous and it lit a torch which changed public perception. This volume is a testimony to the fact that even over twenty years on the implications of that campaign are still being worked through.

INTRODUCTION

This is the fourth volume in the series which has already recorded those country houses, villas and mansions which have been swept away in County Durham and North and East Yorkshire. The authors of this Northumbrian edition have discovered more than one hundred houses that have been demolished within the old county boundaries that existed prior to the 1974 re-organisation and the creation of Tyne and Wear. The principles of inclusion remain the same as in previous volumes. Medieval castles, lost for centuries, have been excluded, although occasionally, as with both Belsay (p.36) and Widdrington (p.67), later additions to the original fortified tower houses have merited inclusion. Houses demolished before 1900 and not rebuilt on the same site are described, as are houses lost since 1900, even when a new house was built on the site. A few houses of particular interest, which survive substantially reduced, such as Eshott (p.45) and Felton (pp.46-47), have also been included.

The architecture of England's most northern county has its own distinctive flavour, seasoned by the proximity of the Border. A turbulent relationship with Scotland which often flared into warfare ensured that fortification was of primary importance long after the inhabitants of counties further south were turning their thoughts to more aesthetic issues. As Thomas Fuller observed in 1662: "one cannot rationally expect fair fabricks here where the vicinity of the Scots made not to build for state but strength". Until the Union of 1603, few in Northumberland were foolhardy enough to leave behind the security of their tower houses or peles to occupy undefended domestic quarters.

Even after the Union, most families were content to add an additional wing to an existing tower rather than build afresh. Thus in these parts the flowering of the country house occurred much later than in the south. The advent of the Civil War during the 1640s, with the Scottish invasion and Parliamentary blockade of the Tyne, served to retard further the development of new architectural forms.

However, by the latter part of the 17th century, isolated examples of country house building were occurring, primarily to the designs of Robert Trollope (d.1686), a stonemason originally from York. Nearer the security of the city, great houses were begun slightly earlier (see Anderson Place, p.8 and Stotes Hall, p.29) but it was not until the 18th century that Northumberland witnessed a sustained proliferation of great houses; the designs of these are often unattributable, indicating the strength of the builder-architect tradition within the county. Major architects, however, known to have been at work are Daniel Garrett (d.1753), James Paine (1717-89), and William Newton (1730-98), the last-named the first truly Northumbrian architect.

Once country house building commenced, powered by mineral and industrial wealth, rising rentals and agricultural improvement, Northumberland proved to be no slouch in the development of architectural style. The Gothic Revival, no doubt due to the influence of the Duke of Northumberland who gothicised Alnwick Castle from 1752, took a firm grasp of the imagination of the county's elite and many houses were transformed into flimsy confections of castellations and crenellations, as their owners sought to outdo their neighbours and create the perfect castle fantasy. The Greek Revival was, similarly, promptly adopted, thanks to the pioneering designs of the gentleman architect Sir Charles Monck at Belsay from 1807, and continued by the work of Northumberland-born John Dobson (1787-1865), who worked for many of those newly enriched by Newcastle's early industrialisation.

The county had, and continues to have, a low population density. Generally, great houses were built on the coastal plain in the eastern half of the county or around centres of population such as Hexham, Alnwick, Morpeth and, of course, Newcastle. Few patrons were brave enough to commission houses in the wilder western reaches, although a Gothic enclave did spring up around Wooler.

The majority of Newcastle's mansion houses were constructed towards the end of the 18th and throughout the 19th centuries as the emergent professions settled in the rural villages surrounding the city, which were not yet part of its sprawl. Early industrialists, merchants, lawyers and surgeons were later replaced with bankers, chemists and, of course, shipbuilders who vied in their attempts to beautify and improve their estates in miniature which ringed the city.

Northumberland has fared better than many in the retention of its mansions, although, as the following pages testify, extensive losses have occurred. *The Architect and Building News* of June 1934 lamented what it referred to as a "Northumbrian tragedy" in which "innumerable country homes ... are succumbing to the combined influence of industrial depression and coal mining operations".

Despite such scaremongering, many of Northumberland's ancient families continue to live in houses commissioned by their forebears; most of the houses of the major aristocracy survive and there are still Charltons at Hesleyside, Ridleys at Blagdon, and Swinburnes at Capheaton. Many more Northumbrian country houses, particularly the smaller classical villas by Newton and Dobson, have proved eminently adaptable for modern living arrangements and survive surrounded by reduced estate holdings. Other houses, such as Callaly Castle, with additions by Trollope, and Belford Hall by Paine, have been saved due to sympathetic conversion into apartments. Longhirst Hall, by Dobson, is now a conference centre and North Dissington Hall, the rebuilt Tillmouth Park, and Linden Hall are hotels.

The situation is bleaker in Newcastle, which, due to the greater pressures of urban expansion, has been less fortunate in the retention of its suburban villas. The majority of the historic houses and mansions in and around the city have disappeared. Those that have survived, have been converted to institutional or educational use, such as Pendower, built for the banker J. W. Pease in about 1867, which is now a teachers' centre, or the former Jesmond Towers, a late Georgian house with substantial Victorian additions, now La Sagesse High School. Benwell Tower, formerly the residence of the Bishop of Newcastle, has been converted into a public house, aptly named "The Mitre". Gosforth House, a fine Palladian composition by Paine, survives in an adulterated form as part of the grandstand for the racecourse, but such survivals are the exception rather than the norm. Little attempt, unfortunately, has been made to convert such properties to art gallery or museum use and, in the one case of Elswick Hall, proved unsuccessful (see pp.17-18).

Sources of evidence for this study have been many and varied. Northumberland is blessed with comprehensive topographical histories, the most notable being those of Wallis of 1769, Mackenzie of 1811 and 1825, and Hodgson (published between 1820 and 1858). Mackenzie also produced a valuable history of Newcastle in 1827. The fifteen-volume *History of Northumberland* (NCH) has also been an invaluable reference source on houses and their patrons. Directories have also been utilised, particularly to identify houses in the first instance and their latter-day owners. Various issues of *Archaeologia Aeliana* and of *Country Life* have been extremely useful, as have the various editions of *Burke's Peerage, Debrett's Peerage and Baronetage* and *Burke's Landed Gentry*. Also helpful have been the Listed Buildings Schedules of the relevant statutory authorities and the "Bygone" series of booklets produced by the Newcastle Central Library (those most useful for our purposes are referred to in the Bibliography). We have also made extensive use of historic local newspapers and maps. The descriptions of the houses in this volume are of necessity too brief to be considered exhaustive but give an overview, albeit selective, of a fascinating subject. The sections which follow each of the principal sequences on Newcastle and Northumberland provide at least an indication of those lost houses not mentioned in the main text (in some cases because a suitable illustration could not be found). It goes without saying that the authors would be pleased to hear of any further information, significant omissions or the whereabouts of photographs not included.

ACKNOWLEDGEMENTS

As with previous books in the series, the authors have made much use of the knowledge and expertise of local historians and enthusiasts, both through published work and personal help. Of these, our principal debt is to Philip Brooks, who so willingly shared the fruits of his very considerable research on the houses (and their owners) of Newcastle and Northumberland. We would also like to record our grateful thanks to Ian Farrier, who made available his extensive research material (and that of his father, the late George N. Farrier) on the important area of Benwell. Also extremely helpful have been Jimmy Donald, a mine of information, as always, on Jesmond and on Newcastle generally, Terry Quinn, on Benwell and Scotswood, and A. Desmond Walton, on the 'west end' and Newbiggin. All of the above have also been very generous with the loan of reproducible and other material; so also have Josephine Briggs, Jim Davidson (from his huge collection of postcards) and Ursula Chatfield, who have provided a great deal of useful information as well. Among those who assisted us with specific points, Marcia Bircham was most helpful in answering questions about Woodhorn, as were Vera Vaggs with reference to Swarland and Tom Corfe on Beacon Grange. We are most grateful to Sir Roy Strong for so willingly writing the foreword and to Russell Baston and Malcolm Donnelly for their photographic expertise. Gary Haley was kindly responsible for the modern map of Northumberland. Thanks are also due to Ian Chilvers for reading the proofs.

Among the many helpful staff of institutions, too numerous to mention all by name, who have provided invaluable help, were those of the Newcastle Central Library (Local Studies Department), the Local Studies Section of North Tyneside Central Library (especially Eric Hollerton), the Northumberland County Record Office, Melton Park and Morpeth, the Tyne & Wear Archives Service, the National Monuments Record at Swindon; also those of the Northumberland County Council Planning Department, especially Liz Williams, for making available their collection of historic photographs. We are also indebted to the Literary and Philosophical Society of Newcastle upon Tyne and to the Society of Antiquaries of Newcastle upon Tyne for permission to reproduce historic material in their collections, as well as to all the persons and organisations specifically mentioned in the Photographic Acknowledgements section below. We should also like to acknowledge the support of the University of Northumbria at Newcastle and the National Monuments Record.

Finally, it should be emphasised that this book would not have been possible without the invaluable contribution of Lavinia Down, who assisted with research and secretarial work and also compiled the index, and the consistent help and encouragement of Edward and Jill Waterson.

PHOTOGRAPHIC ACKNOWLEDGEMENTS

Authors' photograph: fig.25. Capt. A. J. Baker-Cresswell: figs 63, 64, 65. Beamish, North of England Open Air Museum: fig.112. Sir Michael Blake: figs 104, 105, 106. Mrs. Josephine Briggs: figs 6, 7, 47. Mr. P.R.B. Brooks: figs 41, 70, 83, 88, 92, 98. Mrs. Ursula Chatfield: figs 9, 37. Mr. Jim Davidson: figs 4, 14, 17, 39, 43, 49, 51, 61, 68, 71, 80, 81, 94, 95, 96. Newcastle City Libraries and Arts: figs 3, 12, 15, 18, 19, 26, 29, 30, 31, 32, 38, 40, 42, 45, 46, 72, 86, 89, 93. North Tyneside Libraries: figs 5, 23, 50, 58, 97, 108, 109, 110, 113. Northumberland County Council: figs 53, 55, 69, 82, 90, 91. Northumberland County Record Office: frontispiece; figs 16, 48, 56, 85. Philipson's Studios: figs 34, 35. Mr. Terry Quinn: fig.8. Mrs. G. L. Y. Radcliffe: figs 76, 77, 78. The Royal Commission on the Historical Monuments of England (National Monuments Record): figs 10, 11, 20, 21, 27, 28, 33, 54, 57, 59, 60, 73, 84, 99, 100, 101, 102, 103, 107, 114, back cover. Tyne & Wear Archives Service: fig.24. West Newcastle Local Studies and Picture History Collection: figs 22, 87.

Thomas Faulkner
University of Northumbria at Newcastle.

Phoebe Lowery
The National Trust, Northumbria Region.

LOST HOUSES OF NEWCASTLE

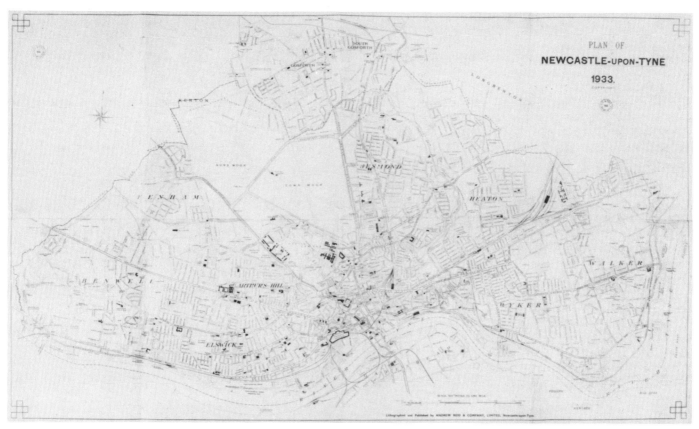

Reid's Map of Newcastle, 1933
(by courtesy of The Literary and Philosophical Society of Newcastle upon Tyne)

ANDERSON PLACE

Anderson Place was Newcastle's most spectacular house, the largest, it is said, in the country within a city wall. Originally the land belonged to the Church but became the property of the merchant Robert Anderson in 1580. On the site of a Friary he built the "Newe House". In 1646 Charles I was kept prisoner here (see p.24). Fig. 1 shows its remarkable 13 acre estate, with Pilgrim Street in the foreground and, at right angles, the 'town wall' on the line of the modern Blackett Street. The house was purchased in 1675 by Sir William Blackett, M.P. for Newcastle and eventual owner of Wallington, Northumberland. Enriched through shipping, coal and lead, he added the vast brick-built wings to the house with modern sash windows which are clearly visible in fig. 2. It was sold in 1782 to George Anderson, a builder, by which time Wallington had passed to the Trevelyans, who already had substantial landholdings in Somerset and wished to rationalise their Northumbrian estates.

George Anderson's son, who had renamed the house, died in 1831 and, due to its position in the centre of what is now modern Newcastle, Anderson Place became a key part of Richard Grainger's scheme to rebuild the city and was consequently demolished in 1834. It stood on or near the site of the present Lloyds Bank in Grey Street.

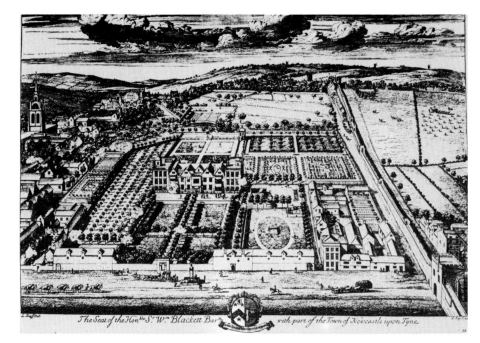

The Seat of the Honble Sr. Wm. Blackett Bart . . . with part of the Town of Newcastle upon Tyne.

Fig. 1 *Anderson Place, Newcastle*

Fig. 2 *Anderson Place, Newcastle*

BEECH GROVE, ELSWICK

This Jacobean-style house (fig. 3) was pulled down in about 1897, at which time it was owned by George Angus, a leather manufacturer. It stood south of Elswick Road, in grounds occupying approximately the site bounded by the present Beech Grove Road, Park Close and Westmorland Road, adjoining those of Elswick Hall. Beech Grove had been the home of Edward Richardson (1805-63), another leather manufacturer, and, in early life, of his son, John Wigham Richardson (see pp.15 and 30). William Mather occupied it in 1861.

Fig. 3 *Beech Grove, Elswick   (Newcastle City Libraries and Arts)*

BENTON HALL

The history of houses in the Longbenton area is confusing because of changes of name. Benton Hall was sometimes known as Little Benton Hall and on other occasions as Benton White House. Mackenzie (1825) appears to refer to it as Benton House. What can be established is that it was built c.1760 (the wings may have been added later) by Thomas Bigge, a coal-owner and brother of William (d. 1758), High Sheriff of Northumberland in 1751. In 1838 it was the residence of Mrs. James Anderson and, after 1858, of the banker John Anthony Woods, although between about 1854 and 1858 the estate was converted into a public Botanical Gardens. The house lay north and west respectively of the present Coast Road and Red Hall Drive; it was unoccupied c.1900-1929 and demolished shortly after this for residential development.

Fig. 4 *Benton Hall, Newcastle   (Mr. Jim Davidson)*

BENTON PARK

Benton Park was built in the late 18th century with projecting wings linked to the main block by curving walls or arcades. It was owned by Dixon Brown and later Dixon Dixon of Longbenton and occupied by the former's son-in-law William Clark of Belford Hall, for whom Dobson in 1813 surveyed the estate (this was adjacent to that of Benton Hall, on the latter's western side, bounded approximately by the present Coast Road, Etherstone Avenue and Red Hall Drive). At this time known as Benton House and later referred to as Red Hall or even Benton Park Hall, it had become by 1838 the residence of John Potts, a coal-owner, and later of Edward Potts, and by 1871 of Edward Liddell (1815-79), formerly of Jesmond Park. It remained in the possession of the Liddells until c.1897, after which it was unoccupied before becoming a Golf Club after the First World War. It was demolished during the 1930s for residential development.

Fig. 5 *Benton Park, Newcastle* *(North Tyneside Central Library)*

BENWELL COTTAGE

Built in 1844 by William Hawthorn, a civil engineer, and sold to the coal-owner J. O. Scott in 1881, from 1906 to 1924 it was occupied by the industrialist Col. William Angus. It was one of many mansions in the then attractive village of Benwell, integrated into the city only in 1904. This house stood on the south side of Ferguson's Lane near the junction with Benwell Lane. Its estate extended to nine acres, the southern boundary having been to the south of what is now Betts Avenue but, during the 1930s, much of this was sold to the Newcastle Corporation for

Fig. 6 *Benwell Cottage, Newcastle* *(Newcastle City Libraries and Arts, © Mrs. Josephine Briggs)*

residential development. In 1925 the Cottage became a young men's hostel of the nearby Royal Victoria School for the Blind and later was used also for civil defence purposes. The remainder of its estate was sold off during the 1950s and the house demolished in 1972 (see fig. 7). Sheltered housing now stands on the site.

Fig. 7 *Benwell Cottage, Newcastle, under demolition*
(Newcastle City Libraries and Arts, © *Mrs. Josephine Briggs)*

BENWELL GRANGE

The Grange was built 1860-63 for Benjamin Carr Lawton, a civil engineer; later owners included George Angus, a gutta-percha merchant and relative of Col. Angus of the Cottage (1872-77), the banker Ralph Brown (c.1878-97) and J. E. McPherson (1897-1914). In 1907 it became a Training School for disabled servicemen and from 1920 to 1954 served as a girls' hostel of the Royal Victoria School for the Blind. It stood in two acres of land off Benwell Lane near the present Hodgkin Park Road, and in 1968 was replaced by flats.

Fig. 8 *Benwell Grange, Newcastle (Mr. Terry Quinn)*

BENWELL HALL

Little trace of Benwell Hall, which was situated on the north side of Ferguson's Lane, west of the junction with Gretna Road, remains today. The only clues to its existence are a few mature trees which were retained as part of the sheltered housing development which occupies the Hall's former site. Most substantial mansions in the North East were constructed of stone, which was easily available from a variety of quarries. Benwell Hall, however, was built of brick, probably during the second half of the 18th century, judging by the architectural style. Later extensions were added during the 19th century, possibly to the designs of Dobson. The original house was symmetrical, two storeys in height and five bays wide with a double string course separating the ground and first floor; the later additions on either side of the original block are clearly discernable (see fig. 9).

William Surtees, son of the Newcastle banker Aubone Surtees and the brother of Bessie Surtees who eloped with John Scott, later Lord Eldon, was resident in the house in the late 18th century. According to Mackenzie, by the 1820s it was occupied by the chemical manufacturer William Cuthbert, who was to commission Dobson to build Beaufront Castle in 1836. Some time afterwards, the Hall became the home of the merchant William Cookson and later of the Liddell family. Cuthbert Liddell, a merchant, passed the estate to his son John Liddell, a colliery owner who was resident in 1873. His son, another John, initially lived at Benwell but moved to Prudhoe Hall in 1897, after having inherited the property from an uncle.

Fig. 9 *Benwell Hall, Newcastle   (Mrs. Ursula Chatfield)*

Fig. 10 *Benwell Hall, Newcastle, from the east   (RCHME, © Crown copyright)*

Benwell Hall was then leased to John Burdon and sold in 1924 to William Bramble. Around this date some of the land was sold off to provide a sports field for Vickers Armstrong which eventually passed to Newcastle United for use as a training ground. William Bramble died in 1948 leaving six daughters, the last of whom died in 1980. Despite considerable public opposition, the house was demolished in 1982 after plans to convert it into executive apartments failed.

Today Benwell reveals little evidence of its previous elegant existence as a sought-after location for the houses of well-to-do gentry and the emergent professions. Mackenzie, describing Benwell in the 1820s, wrote that the village "is extremely rural, and the situation is high, pleasant and healthy, commanding a beautiful and extensive prospect". Benwell is now encompassed by Newcastle and much of it is shabby and run down, a far cry from its hey-day 150 years ago.

Fig. 11 *Benwell Hall, Newcastle, doorcase in first floor room*
(RCHME, © Crown copyright)

BENWELL HOUSE

This was built for John Walker of Wallsend shortly before 1825 on the south side of Benwell Lane. In 1848 it was sold to the tanner Jonathan Priestman, having been let to John Cookson, another industrialist. The historian Mackenzie admired its garden, which was "large and tastefully laid out with a fountain and jet d'eau". In 1879 the house was sold to Edward Bilton and in 1901 to J. Lamb Ltd., brewers, after which it became the Benwell House Hotel. The addition seen in fig. 12 dated from 1937. The Hotel closed in 1968 and the house was demolished in 1972. A Chapel of Rest was built on the site.

Fig. 12 *Benwell House, Newcastle*   *(Newcastle City Libraries and Arts)*

BENWELL PARK

Another example of the popular neo-Elizabethan style, Benwell Park was built in 1852 for the barrister John P. Mulcaster. It lay south of the West Road, between the estates of Pendower House and Condercum House, in four acres near to the line of the Roman Wall. In 1914 the house was sold to the shipowner Leonard Macarthy and about twenty years later to the local builders Hadden & Hillman; they redeveloped the site with an estate of semi-detached houses, called, eponymously, Denhill Park.

Fig. 13 *Benwell Park, Newcastle*

CARVILLE HALL, WALLSEND

Wallsend is now part of Newcastle's eastern sprawl; however, in years gone by it enjoyed a separate existence as a country village. Carville Hall was originally known as Cosyn's House after John Cosyn, a successful Newcastle alderman and cloth merchant who also owned the town house pictured below (fig. 15). He built Cosyn's House, Wallsend, about 1635 and died without issue in 1661. The house passed through several families before it was purchased in the early 18th century by Robert Carr, a prosperous draper from Etal, Northumberland. Carr rebuilt the house, rechristening it Carville. In 1873 the Hall and its estate of 60 acres were purchased by the Quaker shipbuilder John Wigham Richardson of Rye Hill, who used the land to extend his shipyard and construct model cottages for his employees. The Hall was eventually demolished in 1898.

Fig. 14 *Carville Hall, Wallsend*   *(Mr. Jim Davidson)*

Fig. 15 *Cosyn's House, Newcastle*   *(Newcastle City Libraries and Arts)*

COSYN'S HOUSE

A typical example of the merchants' houses which used to stand on the Quayside, in this case immediately east of the Guildhall. By 1840 it had become a public house, being replaced in 1896 by a now-demolished office building. The house had survived remarkably well, with the principal room on the second floor having panelled walls, stuccoed ceiling and magnificent carved overmantel embellished with heraldic arms.

COXLODGE HALL, GOSFORTH

In 1796, Job Bulman, a medical man originally from Gateshead who had made a fortune in India, built Coxlodge Hall and lived in it until his death in 1818. His son Job James immediately tenanted it (Christopher Fenwick occupied it in 1827) and moved into the smaller Coxlodge Cottage (later known as Ashburton Villa). He began to sell off much of his estate and in 1832 sold the Hall and about 30 acres of land to the banker John Anderson, fourth son of John Anderson of Jesmond (see p.23); in 1859, it was purchased by Thomas Hedley, a soap manufacturer. In 1877, the house was burnt down, only to be rebuilt two years later (fig. 16) by the shipbuilder Andrew Leslie, who sold it to John Harper Graham, a wine merchant, in 1894. A later owner was another shipbuilder, Rowland Hodge (c.1910-14). By the 1930s, much of the estate had been sold for suburban development (see fig. 17) but the building, by now a private school, survived until 1939. It was situated on the north side of what is now The Drive, a street running westwards from the southern end of Gosforth High Street and originally the drive to the Hall itself. The stables, now used as offices, and a lodge on the main road, still exist.

Fig. 16 *Coxlodge Hall, Gosforth*   *(Northumberland County Record Office)*

Fig. 17 *Coxlodge Hall, Gosforth, from the air*   *(Mr. Jim Davidson)*

ELSWICK HALL

Originally the Elswick estate was held by the Jennison family, who made their first purchase of land there in 1640. Sir Ralph Jennison, a successful Newcastle merchant, continued to add to his holdings during the Protectorate, buying up several of the surrounding farms. The subsequently-enlarged estate was sold by his great-grandson, who preferred to live at Walworth Castle in Durham.

The purchaser was John Hodgson, an affluent cloth merchant, and a considerable colliery owner along the banks of the Tyne. His father had settled in Newcastle in 1671, the family having originated from Brough in Westmorland. The purchaser's grandson, John Hodgson III, commissioned the rebuilding of Elswick Hall in 1803, the year of his marriage to Sarah Huntley. The father and son partnership William and John Stokoe of Newcastle were chosen as architects. Biographical details for the pair are sketchy, but it is thought that William (d.1802) was probably a builder who branched into architectural design. His son John (1756-1836) is thought to have received at least some sort of architectural training, primarily because of his early and very proficient use of the Greek Doric order in his designs for Newcastle's Moot Hall, begun in 1810.

John Hodgson died in 1820, leaving Elswick to his son, another John, an M.P. for Newcastle and enthusiastic supporter of the development of the city. He sold the estate in 1839 to Richard Grainger, who played the leading role in the development of the city centre during the 1830s. For a short time Grainger made the house his home, as did, in the 1860s, the manufacturer Christian Allhusen, but

Fig. 18 *Elswick Hall, Newcastle*   (*Newcastle City Libraries and Arts*)

Fig. 19 *Elswick Hall, Newcastle, prior to demolition*   (*Newcastle City Libraries and Arts*)

eventually the estate came back on the market for sale as building plots. By this time, Newcastle was rapidly expanding westwards and there was a great need for housing to cater for the employees of the Armstrong Engineering Works.

The sale, however, never went ahead as a number of Newcastle worthies banded together and bought the estate, passing it to the City Council for use as a public park. Elswick Park was opened to the public in 1881. For some years the house was used to display the work of the local sculptor J. G. Lough (1798-1876), designer of the Stephenson monument in Newcastle. Later, however, rising running costs forced the Council to abandon the Hall and it was eventually demolished about 1980 and a swimming pool constructed on the site. Elswick Park survives and was extensively refurbished at the time the house was demolished, re-opening in the year of its centenary to provide much needed recreational space in the city's economically depressed 'west end'.

Fig. 20 *Elswick Hall, Newcastle, south entrance hall foyer (RCHME, © Crown copyright)*

Fig. 21 *Elswick Hall, Newcastle, ground floor south-east room*　　(*RCHME, © Crown copyright*)

ELSWICK HOUSE

This early 19th-century villa stood on the south side of Elswick Road, west of the Elswick Hall estate. In 1873 it was occupied by Clement Lister, in 1874 by W. H. Darnell and from c.1887 by the prominent Methodist Sir William Haswell Stephenson (1836-1918). He was Mayor of Newcastle seven times and in 1903 had one of the mayoral barges placed in the garden of his house, which in the 1930s was used as a children's home. After the Second World War it became St. Anne's Convent High School; this closed in 1983 and a Marie Curie Centre now occupies the site.

Fig. 22 *Elswick House, Newcastle   (West Newcastle Local Studies)*

FOREST HALL

Forest Hall gave its name to the suburb now occupying the area of its very extensive estate. Woodside Court, in Woodside Crescent, off Westcroft Road, was built on the site of the Hall, which was demolished in 1962. The western portion of this (on the left in fig. 23) incorporated part of the original medieval tower, although the crenellations were modern. Richard Wilson (1695-1759) was probably responsible for building the five-bay central block, the eastern wing being a later addition. During the 19th century the Hall was frequently tenanted (e.g. in 1834 to John Straker, a coalowner), but the Wilsons re-occupied it c.1910-56.

Fig. 23 *Forest Hall, Newcastle   (North Tyneside Central Library)*

"THE GABLES", ELSWICK

This Tudor-Gothic mansion, later known as Hopedean House, was typical of the gentlemen's residences being built during the mid-19th century in the 'west end' of Newcastle. Elswick was incorporated into the city in 1835; it rapidly became industrialised, its population growing from 3,500 in 1851 to 60,000 in 1901. The original medieval village had centred on the area of the present Elswick Park (see pp.17-18). Later, prominent landowners included the Jennisons, the Hodgsons and the Ordes. "The Gables" stood on the corner of Gloucester Road and Elswick Road. It was built by the Richardsons (a close-knit Quaker family who owned the nearby Elswick Leather Works in Water Street) and occupied by David Richardson. "The Gables" survived until 1996 (see fig. 25) having been, since the 1920s, a private nursing home and, latterly, a Salvation Army hostel. Meanwhile, the leather works had closed down in the 1970s, when most of Elswick was being redeveloped. Near "The Gables", in Gloucester Terrace, were South Ashfield, also owned by the Richardsons, and North Ashfield, occupied in 1873 by Sir B. C. Browne and c.1897-1914 by Sir Joseph Baxter Ellis, another Mayor of Newcastle.

Fig. 24 *"The Gables", Elswick*   *(Tyne & Wear Archives)*

Fig. 25 *"The Gables", Elswick, under demolition*   *(Authors' photograph)*

HEATON HALL

Heaton Hall was re-faced by William Newton for Sir Matthew White Ridley in the late 1770s. Essentially classical, it became a wonderful example of the pastry-cook Gothic so prevalent in 18th-century Northumberland. Newton's first attempt at Gothic architecture was probably the equally flimsy-looking Kielder Castle, a shooting-box for the Duke of Northumberland, completed in 1772. Newton was known to Sir Matthew from at least 1774, since the baronet was part of the committee set up to promote the building of the new Assembly Rooms in Newcastle; Newton was appointed architect and as a result became favoured by the Northumbrian elite.

The White Ridleys represented an amalgamation of the families of two of Newcastle's early entrepreneurs, Matthew White and Richard Ridley, who became enriched through shrewd business calculation and the opportunities presented by the city's early industrialisation. The Heaton estate originally belonged to the Ridleys; Blagdon, near Stannington, Northumberland, to the Whites. The White line, however, ended with an heiress who married Matthew Ridley; their son Sir Matthew White Ridley inherited Blagdon in 1763 and Heaton in 1778. The alterations, begun shortly afterwards, were completed by 1783. As an engraving of that year shows, the house, built originally in 1713, sported battlemented towers and a crenellated parapet, thus giving it the fashionable "castle air" (fig. 26 and front cover).

During the second half of the 19th century the house was owned by the Potter family. Their ancestor Addison Potter began as a fitter with W. G.

Fig. 26 *Heaton Hall, Newcastle*   *(Newcastle City Libraries and Arts)*

Fig. 27 *Heaton Hall, Newcastle, drawing room*
(RCHME © Crown copyright)

Armstrong but worked his way up to become a Director, establishing his descendants at Heaton. In the 1890s some of the land surrounding the house was sold off for the creation of Armstrong Park. Heaton was demolished in 1933. The Ridleys are still at Blagdon, where in the grounds stands a (now roofless) circular temple (fig. 28), also by Newton, brought from Heaton as a last reminder of a house now lost.

Fig. 28 *Heaton Hall, Newcastle, garden rotunda (RCHME © Crown copyright)*

JESMOND GROVE

From 1802 until his death James Losh (1762-1833), Recorder of Newcastle, lived in this house. It stood west of Jesmond Dene Road, above the ruins of St. Mary's Chapel, which lay within its grounds. John Dobson worked on the house in 1817, but it would appear to have been gothicised in the mid-19th century, probably for Matthew and Thomas Anderson. In the early 1900s, the Grove was owned by the brewer W. B. Reid and occupied by Henry Armstrong; from 1916 until its demolition in 1927 it was a boarding house for the Church High School.

Fig. 29 *Jesmond Grove, Newcastle*   *(Newcastle City Libraries and Arts)*

JESMOND MANOR HOUSE

Formerly known as Jesmond House, this lay just north of where the present Manor House Road joins Grosvenor Road, having been rebuilt by William Coulson in 1720 on the site of Nicholas Grenville's 12th-century house. In 1809 it was purchased by John Anderson (1757-1829) who "much adorned and beautified it" (Mackenzie), and in 1887 by Col. Coulson, who later sold it to James Laing. Subsequently occupied by Alfred Cochrane and then by the shipbuilder Sir Herbert Babington Rowell, the house was later used as a nursing home and demolished in 1929. Its splendid iron gates were re-erected, only recently, as a feature of the Byker Wall housing development.

Fig. 30 *Jesmond Manor House, Newcastle*   (*Newcastle City Libraries and Arts*)

KENTON LODGE

Kenton was a mining village, largely redeveloped during the 1960s. The Lodge stood at its south-east corner at the junction of Kenton Road and Grandstand Road. It was built in 1795 for the coal-owner John Graham Clarke, grandfather of Elizabeth Barrett Browning. From 1810 to 1836 it was the seat of John Brandling, and for the next three years was occupied by Sir John Walsham, a Poor Law Commissioner. Later occupiers were mainly farmers. In 1908 it was replaced by the present neo-Georgian house, built for the paint manufacturer Max Holzapfel.

Fig. 31 *Kenton Lodge, Newcastle, c.1795*   (*Newcastle City Libraries and Arts*)

KENTON MANOR

Formerly known as Manor House Farm, this curiously asymmetrical house was situated on the north side of Kenton Lane at Kenton Bar and was demolished c.1960. It probably dated from about 1700 — its main gables had triangular 'spandrel-stones' typical of this period of Northumbrian masonry — but incorporating older parts. On the western gable was an oriel window and a tympanum, carved in low relief with the date 1616. From about 1897 to 1921 the house was occupied by the Potts family.

*Fig. 32 Kenton Manor, Newcastle
(Newcastle City Libraries and Arts)*

KING CHARLES'S HOUSE

This was situated in Shield Street, overlooking the 'Shield Field', where Charles I was allowed to play 'goff' while imprisoned in Newcastle during the Civil War (see p.8), resting at the house. It was demolished in 1960 as part of the replanning of Newcastle; the area was redeveloped with high-rise flats, typifying the belief in the utopian possibilities of modern architecture at this time. King Charles's House was threatened with demolition in 1838 and its future was again uncertain in 1917 when its owner, Alderman Sir Richard Walter Plummer, presented it to the Council in order to ensure its preservation.

*Fig. 33 King Charles's House, Newcastle
(RCHME © Crown Copyright)*

LOW GOSFORTH HOUSE

More recently known as Low Gosforth Court, this was originally part of the Brandling Estate; situated near the Northumberland County Record Office, it was demolished in the early 1970s (see frontispiece). During the first half of the 19th century it was occupied by Robert William Brandling (1775-1849), younger brother of the Rev. Ralph Henry Brandling of Gosforth House. At the sale of the Brandling property in 1852, Low Gosforth was purchased by Joseph Laycock for £28,600; its estate of 287 acres included the ruins of North Gosforth Chapel, standing near the drive. Mr. Laycock demolished the existing house (date unknown) and erected a new one, in the mid-1850s, which was destroyed by fire in 1878 and rebuilt (see figs. 34 and 35). He was succeeded in 1881 by his son Brig.-Gen. Sir Joseph Frederick Laycock. By 1894 the house had become the residence of James A. Woods (son of John Anthony Woods of Benton Hall), who later moved to Swarland Park (see p.60), and later of Brodie Cochrane and Sir Alfred E. Bell. The estate became incorporated into the Melton Park residential development, east of the Great North Road, stables and other outbuildings being converted to residential use.

Fig. 34 *Low Gosforth House, Newcastle*   *(Philipson's Studios)*

Fig. 35 *Low Gosforth House, Newcastle, interior prior to demolition*   *(Philipson's Studios)*

THE MANSION HOUSE

It was built in 1691 at a cost of £6,000. Accommodating the Mayor, and visiting judges, it was opulently furnished and had a terrace and private quay; the curious low portico was added in about 1825. It stood on the Quayside, near the site of the present Copthorne Hotel, an area which became unsuitably industrial during the 18th and 19th centuries. The abolition of the old Corporation in 1836 sealed its fate; a year later it was controversially auctioned off with all its contents and subsequently used as a timber warehouse. It was destroyed by fire on 6th October 1895.

Fig. 36 *The Mansion House, Newcastle*

146-148 NEWGATE STREET

Standing on the east side of Newgate Street, approximately opposite St. Andrew's church, this was another victim of Newcastle's post-war redevelopment. Its early owners are unknown but it appears to have been reconstructed during the 18th century, while retaining an earlier inscription dated 1634. Some of its rooms had ceilings decorated with Jacobean 'strap-work'. It became a public house known as "The Masons' Arms" (later "Bourgognes") before being demolished in 1972.

Fig. 37 *146-148 Newgate Street, Newcastle*   *(Mrs. Ursula Chatfield)*

PICTON HOUSE

Designed by Dobson c.1825, it was part of a development laid out along New Bridge Street following the construction of a bridge over the Pandon Dene. Of this, only the architect's own house (now a night club) and some houses east of the present Falconar Street survive. Picton House, demolished in 1970 (fig. 38), was at the southern end of Picton Place near the junction with New Bridge Street and Oxford Street. In 1860 it was the residence of George Mennell and for many years survived as a railway ticket office and later as an employment exchange.

Fig. 38 *Picton House, Newcastle, prior to demolition* *(Newcastle City Libraries and Arts)*

POINT PLEASANT HOUSE, WALLSEND

Situated south of what was the main road to Tynemouth near the present Point Pleasant Terrace, in an estate stretching from the riverside to Wallsend village green, it was owned by James Muncaster the elder of Wallsend Hall. From his son it was bought by William Clark, who sold it to William Losh. In 1822 Alice, the latter's eldest daughter, was married to James Anderson, the third son of John Anderson (see p.23) and they occupied Point Pleasant until 1837. Later owners were John Grace, John Straker, John Coutts, Thomas Jobling and, after 1879, the Wallsend Slipway Company; Robert Wallis lived there c.1910-21.

Fig. 39 *Point Pleasant House, Wallsend* *(Mr. Jim Davidson)*

THE RED HOUSE, WALLSEND

This was one of several houses, including The Grange (dem. 1913) and the White House (dem. 1910), on the old village green, to the east of Station Road, in this case on the north-west side. It was probably built c.1770 for Henry Waters, a 'hostman', or his successor William. Their family occupied the house until 1799, when it was sold to John Walker (d.1822), then to Francis Peacock, a coal-owner, and in 1858 to John Allen, another industrialist. In the 1880s it became a children's home, being replaced in 1897 by Hawthorn Villas and Park Villas, also now pulled down.

Fig. 40 *The Red House, Wallsend*   (*Newcastle City Libraries and Arts*)

SCOTSWOOD TOWER

In 1367 Richard Scot began to make a park out of his wood west of Benwell — this is the origin of the name Scotswood. Little is known of this curious Victorian house, apparently built on to an ancient tower. In 1873 it was occupied by W. J. Browne and in 1912 by a Miss A. Hall. It stood on the right hand side of Denton Road, going towards the Tyne, near the present Sports and Social Club; across the road was Scotswood House, the home of Mrs. Elizabeth Lister in 1855, Nathaniel Grace from 1858, and later of the Weightman family. Both houses were demolished in the early 1970s.

Fig. 41 *Scotswood Tower, Newcastle*   (*Mr. P. R. B. Brooks*)

STOTES HALL

This ancient house stood on the east side of Jesmond Dene Road, opposite Cavendish Road, and was demolished in the late 1950s. Allotments now adjoin the site. Above its front door were the arms of the Newcastle Merchant Adventurers, dated 1607, when the house was rebuilt by either Robert Gibson or Robert Greenwell. T-shaped in plan, having hall and kitchen in the main arm, with an additional north wing, it was probably the first non-fortified manor in Northumberland to be constructed outside town or city walls. In 1658 it was purchased (and renamed) by Sir Richard Stote, a Commissioner for the county who died in 1682, and in 1756 by Sir Robert Bewick and John Craster; for a few years it was kept as a school by the mathematician Dr. Charles Hutton. Stotes Hall assumed something like its final appearance (fig. 42) when modernised by the Shields family in the early 19th century. Later occupants included the ship-owner Fife J. Scott (in 1873), Robert Johnson, John B. Dodds, and, in the early 1900s, C. W. Fairweather, General Manager of the Electricity Supply Company. From about 1914 it was occupied by Sir Alfred Appleby, the Newcastle Coroner, before being sold in 1927 to Miss Doris Cowper, who renovated it. Latterly the Hall was used by the St. John's Ambulance Brigade; it retained some unpretentious Jacobean stone fireplaces, and some mullioned windows in the end gable walls.

Fig. 42 *Stotes Hall, Newcastle*   *(Newcastle City Libraries and Arts)*

Fig. 43 *Stotes Hall, Newcastle, interior*   *(Mr. Jim Davidson)*

WEST ACRES, BENWELL

In 1888 Sir Benjamin C. Browne, Mayor of Newcastle two years earlier, purchased this Victorian mansion from another Benwell resident Percy Westmacott. Within ten years it was suffering from subsidence and in 1930 was sold to the builder Harry Kindred who redeveloped the site with the present West Acres Crescent estate. West Acres House faced east in seven acres of ornamental and wooded gardens on the southern side of the West Road, bounded also by Fox and Hounds Lane to the east, and by playing fields to the south and west. An attractive lodge stood on the main road (see p.31).

Fig. 44 *West Acres House, Newcastle*

WINGROVE HOUSE, FENHAM

In the Middle Ages the township was owned by the Knights Templar and later by the Riddells and then the Ordes. By 1900 the Fenham and Wingrove estates were being sold off for building purposes. Thus Wingrove House (along with the nearby Wingrove Cottage and, further to the north-west, Fenham White House) was demolished in about 1903, when its owner since 1866, the shipbuilder John Wigham Richardson (1837-1908), retired to Stocksfield. It stood on the north side of Westgate Road, just to the west of the junction with the present Wingrove Road. It had been built c.1847 for Lawrence Hewison, a corn factor.

Fig. 45 *Wingrove House, Newcastle   (Newcastle City Libraries and Arts)*

MORE LOST HOUSES OF NEWCASTLE

The city's most dynamic phases of development occurred during the 19th century, when many earlier houses disappeared, and in the period after about 1960 when most of the mansions built during the previous period of expansion were removed. Suburban development between the Wars had also taken its toll of these. By about 1700 the residential and mercantile character of Newcastle was becoming established. Pictured in Corbridge's Map of 1723 are numerous houses with plain classical facades and, sometimes, shaped gables. Nearly all of these have disappeared, including **Hills Court** (the home of Richard Hill) and **Wellington Place** (occupied by Joseph Bainbridge), both in Pilgrim Street, Thomas Anderson's house, on the site of the Literary and Philosophical Society Library, and the Derwentwater residence (see p.44) in the area of Bell's Court on the west side of Newgate Street (demolished c.1850).

Other casualties have been Northumberland House in the Close, the **'King's Manor'** (formerly the Austin Friary), **Forth House**, and **Westmorland Place** (the Neville residence), all victims of railway development. **Vicarage House** stood in Westgate Road, and there were many curious old houses in nearby Low Friar Street, such as **Dolphin House**. In the same area was **Cross House**, a brick mansion of c.1700 re-faced in the late 19th century and demolished c.1912; it was replaced by a commercial building of the same name. "**Billy Purvis's House**", on the Quayside, was also built of brick, but perhaps a few decades later; it was demolished c.1960. On the fringes of the city was **Byker Manor**, just west of the junction of the present

Fig. 46 *West Acres House, Newcastle, the lodge*   (*Newcastle City Libraries and Arts*)

Bothal Street and Brook Street. In 1730 it was the seat of Edward Collingwood and, in earlier times, of the Dent family.

The work in Newcastle of the city's major architect, John Dobson, has not fared well. Gone is his house of c.1825 for David Cram at the eastern end of Ellison Place, a dignified street truncated by the building of the central motorway (east). Mackenzie described it as "the most chaste and elegant specimen of masonry". Later, around 1850, Dobson closed the street with **Gresham Place**, for the coal-owner James Morrison, sadly also lost.

As we have seen, no area of Newcastle has suffered more than the 'west end'. Additional losses here include: **Benwell Grove**, **Benwell Lodge**, **Benwell Mission House**, **Benwell Old House**, **Condercum House**, **Enfield Lodge**, **High Cross House**, **Oakfield**, **Paradise House** and **South Benwell House**. The last-named, demolished early in the present century, stood near the corner of Atkinson Road and Scotswood Road and was occupied by the coal-owner William Cochrane Carr and, in the 1870s, by the French family. Nearby, in a

typically idyllic setting, was **Paradise House**, dating back to at least the early 18th century. **Benwell Grove** was designed by Dobson in 1816, south of Westgate Road in the area of the present Normount Gardens and Benwell Grove Road. By 1825 it was the residence of Anthony Clapham, a soap manufacturer, and later of the barrister H. C. Cooke. Before its demolition c.1914 it was occupied by Captain Edward Lloyd. Opposite was **Gloucester Lodge**, the residence in the early 19th century of a Mrs. Laidler. In the area of St. Cuthbert's School, was **Benwell Lodge**, built c.1760 by Robert Shafto and later the seat of Robert Pearson, a solicitor (in the 1820s), James Graham Clarke (in 1838), Edward Whitfield, a shipowner (c.1851), and of John S. Challoner (c.1855-97); it was pulled down in 1962.

Condercum House was a Victorian mansion on the west side of Condercum Road, demolished to make way for a special school. It was the home of Col. Dwyer, a Director of the Armstrong Works, and, in the 1880s, of Thomas E. Crawhall; it was later occupied by

William Cochrane Carr and the ship-owner J. F. Weidner. Adjacent to this were **Condercum Villa**, the earlier home of T. E. Crawhall, and **Oakfield**, residence of Col. Oliver Selby and then of J. G. Hicks.

High Cross House was designed c.1830 by Dobson, and occupied by R. T. Atkinson, a mining engineer whose daughter married Sir B. C. Browne (see p.30) and later by T. H. Burnett. In 1871 John Phillips, a solicitor, lived there, as later did Hugh Crawford-Smith M.P., before its demolition c.1907. Its site was that now bordered by St. John's Road, Caroline Street, Armstrong Road and Elswick Road, immediately to the west of which stood **Enfield Lodge**, in the late 19th century the residence of J. G. Burdon.

Benwell Mission House (fig. 47) on Benwell Lane, built 1820, served also as a Mission Hall and later a Board School before being demolished c.1943. Also on Benwell Lane was **Benwell Old House**, an early 18th-century mansion rebuilt c.1838. Its owners included Joseph Straker (c.1858-73), A. S. Carr, Ralph Cromwell Gregg and the Thirlwell family. Latterly it was a children's nursery before being demolished c.1955.

On the north side of the city, the Sandyford area contained **Goldspink Hall**, **Jesmond Vale House** and **Sandyford House**, all dating from the first half of the 19th century and demolished c.1901, c.1939 and c.1895 respectively. **Goldspink Hall**, the residence of, among others, Robert Clayton and later C. H. Young, overlooked the Ouseburn on the site of the junction of the present Springbank Road and Greystoke Gardens. **Jesmond Vale House** was to the south-east, at the bottom of Goldspink Lane, and **Sandyford House**, the seat of the Naters family, lay behind their large brewery on Sandyford Road in

Fig. 47 *Benwell Mission House, Newcastle* *(Mrs. Josephine Briggs)*

the area of Grantham Road. Also on Sandyford Road stood **Sandyford Villa**, later renamed **Sandyford House**. For a time it was the Roman Catholic Bishop's residence and later become a girls' hostel. This late 19th-century house was demolished c.1970.

In Benton an important casualty was **Benton Lodge**, a Victorian residence standing south of what is now Benton Park Road, close to the junction of the present Benton Lodge Avenue and Thropton Avenue; in 1887 it was occupied by Miss Elizabeth Anderson and later by an accountant, Alfred Carr. **Benton Grange** was, in the mid-19th century, the seat of Matthew Liddell.

In Jesmond, additional lost houses were: **Cuttersfield House**, on the north side of Hutton Terrace; **Jesmond Dean**, Lord Armstrong's residence in Jesmond Dene Road (dem. c.1930); **Jesmond Park** (c.1900); **St. George's Vicarage**, Osborne Road, an Arts and Crafts design of 1888 by T. R. Spence (c.1965); **St. Mary's Mount**, the Rev. Edward Moises's early 19th-century villa near the present Arm-

strong Bridge — opposite this was '**Wellburn**', built by the paint manufacturer W. H. Holmes in about 1883 (c.1933); **Broomfield Tower**, and **South Jesmond House**, in the Minories (c.1910); **West Jesmond House**, the residence of the brewer T. W. Lovibond, on the corner of Osborne Road and Osborne Avenue, and, to the south, '**Tyneholme**', both on the site of the present Nuffield Hospital. **Jesmond Park** was designed by Dobson in 1828 for the solicitor Armorer Donkin (1779-1851), on an elevated site near the junction of the present Kimberley and Lansdowne Gardens. It was later owned by Edward Liddell, James Morrison and J. G. Hoare.

Finally, mention should be made of **Roseworth House**, Gosforth, situated east of the Great North Road in the area of the present Roseworth Avenue and Crescent. Built in 1832 by the Rev. Walker, it was purchased five years later by the coal-owner John Carr, enlarged by his son in 1875, and demolished in the early 1900s, at which time it was the residence of H. P. Gurney, Principal of Armstrong College.

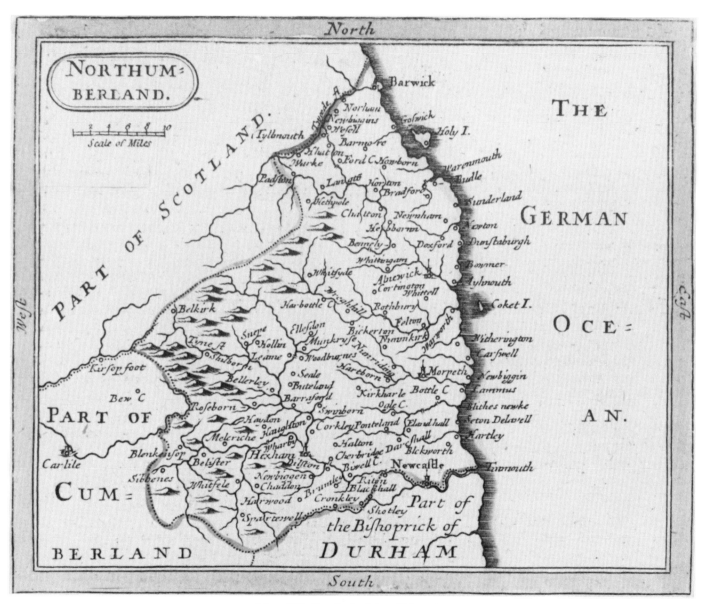

Map of Northumberland, late 18th century

BANK HOUSE

Bank House, near Acklington, was demolished in 1957. Robert Tate, a member of the Alnwick Company of Skinners and Glovers, purchased a farmhouse and the land surrounding it prior to 1782. His son John inherited in 1795 and decided to enlarge the house. The end result was a compact, typically Northumbrian country house. The design of the re-fronted mansion points towards the Newcastle architect William Newton, who was responsible for many similar houses. It may be that he designed Bank House shortly before his death in 1798, although it was not completed until 1799, as commemorated by the rainwater heads which bore the inscription "IT1799".

Fig. 48 *Bank House, near Acklington* *(Northumberland County Record Office)*

BEACON GRANGE (HOUSE)

This appears on Armstrong's Map of Northumberland of 1769. It stood about a mile south of Hexham on the road to Newbiggin. In the 1820s it was the property of S. P. Maughan and occupied by M. W. Carr. It is also said to have been the residence of the Gibsons of Stonecroft, who may have built the house. By 1834, it had been sold to the Rev. W. J. D. Waddilove, from whom it descended after 1879 to Admiral Charles Waddilove. In 1905 it was the residence of the railway engineer Charles A. Harrison and in 1921 of Foster Armstrong.

Fig. 49 *Beacon Grange, near Hexham* *(Mr. Jim Davidson)*

BEACONSFIELD HOUSE, CULLERCOATS

The coal-owner and philanthropist John Henry Burn built this seafront villa in about 1882 at the high cost of £35,000. Near St. George's Church, at the Cullercoats end of Tynemouth Promenade, it was named after Lord Beaconsfield. Mr. Burn died in 1898 although his widow continued in residence until 1922, when it became a Dr. Barnardo's Children's Home. In 1953, Beaconsfield was purchased by Tynemouth Council for use as a convalescent home and was demolished in 1959, although redevelopment plans made at the time were never implemented.

Fig. 50 *Beaconsfield House, Cullercoats* (*North Tyneside Central Library*)

BELLSHILL

Between 1774 and 1789 the Adderstone Estate was sold off and John Pratt purchased 798 acres, including property at Bellshill, for £8,300; the mansion was probably built around this time. He occupied it until 1830, when his heirs sold it to John Church, brother-in-law of P. J. Selby (see p.65). Later Bellshill was owned by Dr. William Selby-Church and tenanted to Maj.-Gen. Bell (in 1887), Capt. R. J. Atkinson-Sharp (c.1894-97) and Miss Grey (1902). Later occupiers included Edward Dove (1910) and Clive Branfoot (1920s). Bellshill stood west of the A1 in a wooded estate (much of which was sold off in the 1920s), and was demolished after the Second World War.

Fig. 51 *Bellshill, near Adderstone* (*Mr. Jim Davidson*)

BELSAY CASTLE

Sir Charles Middleton Monck's Belsay Hall, begun in 1807, survives. However, its predecessor, a 14th-century tower-house with additions of the early 17th, and 18th centuries, is now a roofless ruin standing some distance away and much changed from the Buck engraving of 1728 (fig. 52), which also shows the strict formality of the extensive garden around the house.

First recorded as being in the possession of the Middleton family in 1270, the tower was probably constructed at the end of the 14th century. An unfortified wing was added in 1614 by Thomas Middleton and commemorated by an inscription above the porch, making it a very early example of unfortified domestic architecture in Northumberland. Whereas at Callaly Castle the tower house was re-fenestrated and re-faced in the 18th century and thus brought into harmony with latter additions, the Middletons had no such aesthetic notions; they left their tower-house unaltered, preferring simply to add on an additional wing with the more graceful proportions demanded by Georgian England.

The modern view of the Castle (fig. 53) shows little trace of the Georgian wing, which was further complemented by an elegant stable block which still survives. The central block remains, although it was remodelled in 1862, many years after the family had moved into the starkly Grecian new Hall.

Fig. 52 *Belsay Castle and Old Hall, Northumberland, by S. and N. Buck, 1728 (detail)*

Fig. 53 *Belsay Castle and Old Hall, Northumberland (Northumberland County Council)*

BIDDLESTONE HALL

Situated 800 feet above sea level overlooking the Coquet Valley, Biddlestone was said to have provided Sir Walter Scott with the inspiration for Osbaldeston House in *Rob Roy*. The Selbys became established in the area very early; the estate is said to have been in the possession of this Roman Catholic family for 700 years. Originally a tower-house, Biddlestone was rebuilt c.1796.

Thomas Selby had succeeded to the estate in 1787. Like many Northumbrian architectural patrons of the time, he had married an heiress, whose fortune, in conjunction with rising agricultural rents, allowed him to build a house of very grandiose proportions. It had a starkly plain exterior relieved only by a Tuscan porch (fig. 55). With a dining room of 27′ x 20′, a drawing room and library each 31′ x 21′, a billiard room of a massive 43′ x 22′ and a total of thirteen bedrooms, Biddlestone certainly catered for the large families of the day.

Much altered by Dobson around 1820 for Walter Selby, the Hall, grounds, home farm, and other associated buildings, were withdrawn from the 1914 sale having reached a price of only £11,000. The brewing magnate Farquhar Deuchar lived at Biddlestone from 1925 and the house was used as a convalescent home during the Second World War. It was demolished in 1957. The small separate chapel survives.

Fig. 54 *Biddlestone Hall, Northumberland*   (*RCHME © Crown copyright*)

Fig. 55 *Biddlestone Hall, Northumberland, detail of porch*   (*Northumberland County Council*)

BOTHALHAUGH

This enormous privately-owned rectory was testimony to the wealth and status of the Victorian clergyman. Built in 1880, it was a picturesque red brick assemblage, standing above the river to the east of Bothal village; it contained hydraulic services which opened the principal internal doors when they were approached. Its most famous resident was the Hon. and Rev. William Charles Ellis, son of Lord Howard de Walden and Rector of Bothal from 1861 to 1923. In 1885 he initiated the creation of a separate parish for Ashington. He was also a celebrated horticulturalist.

Fig. 56 *Bothalhaugh, Northumberland*   *(Northumberland County Record Office)*

BROOME PARK

Broome Park, six miles from Alnwick, was purchased by Thomas Burrell in 1658. His descendant Bryan Burrell inherited the estate in 1751 and it is probable that the house was given the appearance shown in fig. 57 during his period of ownership, which continued until 1806.

Stylistic evidence points once more in the direction of William Newton. Burrell acted as High Sheriff for the County in 1768. Newton was patronised by many holding the office of Sheriff, who often reinforced their social position by altering or rebuilding their country seat. Dobson altered the house in 1829 for William Burrell, another member of the family to become Sheriff. The house was demolished in 1953.

Fig. 57 *Broome Park, near Edlingham*   *(RCHME © Crown copyright)*

CHIRTON HOUSE, NORTH SHIELDS

Chirton was a mining village about a mile west of North Shields. Chirton House stood south-west of Hawkeys Lane, north of the present Waterville Road. It was sold in 1876 and demolished in 1899; a Co-operative store was erected on the site. It had been built in 1693 by Winifred Milbourne on the site of an older mansion. In the late 18th century it was the residence of Edward Collingwood (d.1783) and his son, also Edward (d.1805); it then descended to the latter's cousin, Admiral Lord Collingwood (1748-1810), who never lived at Chirton, although his wife and daughters did, and subsequently to the Admiral's brother, John.

Fig. 58 *Chirton House, North Shields*   *(North Tyneside Central Library)*

COWPEN GROVE, BLYTH

Cowpen Grove was one of several Georgian houses on Cowpen Road (this was on the south side, no. 382), including Chase House (no. 485) and Cowpen House, all demolished when the area was redeveloped after the 1960s. The Grove dated from c.1750. In 1897 it is recorded as being the residence of Charles Alderson, solicitor, in 1910 of Christopher Baldwin, and in the 1920s of Leopold Fothergill, a surgeon. In its latter days (see fig.59) its splendid estate of lawns and woods had become reduced almost to nothing; the house itself retained some fine classical interiors.

Fig. 59 *Cowpen Grove, Northumberland*   *(RCHME © Crown copyright)*

COWPEN HALL, BLYTH

Cowpen was a mining village about a mile west of Blyth; the river remained navigable at this point, facilitating the export of coal. The Widdringtons and the Delavals had been prominent landowners in these parts, the latter having occupied a mansion house north of Cowpen Road, on the south side of which Cowpen Hall was situated, north of the present Patterdale Road and on the axis of Cowpen Hall Road. The Hall was probably built in 1720 by Peter Potts, a skinner and glover of Newcastle. What must have been an earlier mansion on the site, shown on a tithe map of 1719, was described four years earlier as "a handsome seat, built with brick with a square tower in ye middle and good garden on ye south" (NCH, ix, p.341); Cowpen Hall as illustrated here was, of course, built of fine ashlar stone. In 1725 Mr. Potts sold it for £5,700 to Stephen Mitford of the Inner Temple, from whom it was purchased by Henry Sidney, another lawyer, four years later. The Sidneys owned Cowpen Hall until the early 20th century. One of the last of them, also called Henry, was a solicitor and coal-owner with mines near Newbiggin-by-the-Sea; a member of his family also owned Cowpen House. Later recorded owners of the Hall were Talbot Hassell, in the 1920s, and Muriel Petrie (in 1945).

Fig. 60 *Cowpen Hall, Northumberland, north elevation*
(RCHME © Crown copyright)

Fig. 61 *Cowpen Hall, Northumberland, from the south*
(Mr. Jim Davidson)

CRESSWELL HALL

The Cresswell family were recorded as possessing lands at Cresswell from the 12th century onwards. The rectangular tower house, which still survives as a roofless ruin, was probably constructed towards the end of the 14th century and shortly after 1749 was converted into a "very convenient and extensive family residence" (fig.62) by William Cresswell, who added a substantial classical wing. The subsequently-improved mansion was advertised to be let in 1772 and was tenanted by several families throughout the later 18th, and 19th centuries, losing its "wonted trimness" to such a degree that the modern additions were demolished in 1845.

The Cresswells themselves appear to have lived at their Woodhorn residence during this period (see p.67). In 1781 the male line ceased with the death of John Cresswell who left twin daughters as his co-heiresses. Frances Cresswell married Francis Easterby, who purchased her sister Catherine's share of the estate, and took Cresswell as his surname. Their son was born in 1788 and christened Addison after his aunt Elizabeth Addison (née Cresswell) who left him considerable land holdings on her death in 1807. Addison Cresswell was clearly a fortunate man. His wife Elizabeth Reed was also an heiress, inheriting a substantial fortune on the death of her cousin, John Baker. The Baker surname was consequently adopted by the Cresswells, making them the Baker Cresswells.

Addison John Baker Cresswell was thus not only possessed of an impressive collection of names but also of a very large fortune and estate. In keeping with the times, he invested that fortune in the

Fig. 62 *Cresswell Tower and Mansion, Northumberland*

Fig. 63 *Cresswell Hall, Northumberland*   (*RCHME © Capt. A. J. Baker-Cresswell*)

building of an imposing mansion, begun in 1821, the year he was High Sheriff for the County. Designs for the new house were drawn up by the London architect, John Shaw, but the construction was supervised by John Green of Newcastle. Cresswell Hall took four years to complete and was described by John Hodgson as a "magnificent structure". Its design was directly influenced by Sir Charles Monck's Belsay Hall. Shaw visited Belsay while it was still under construction in 1811 and ten years later he employed a similar design at Cresswell.

The entrance front (fig.63) duplicated Monck's two giant columns in antis and the otherwise stark facade was relieved only by antae at the angles and pilaster strips either side of the two pedimented ground floor windows. Internally, Shaw copied Monck's top-lit central hall (see fig.64) which stretched to the full height of the house, although he altered the position of the stairs themselves, using a double flight to first floor level. As at Belsay, the principal reception rooms were placed to the south for maximum light, and the kitchen and other offices to the north. Shaw, however, came up with an ingenious plan to screen the offices from view, employing a 16-column colonnade which curved outwards from the north-east corner of the house, connecting the terrace which ran along the east front with the conservatory (see fig.66). Hodgson noted that even in the winter, the temperature in the house seldom dropped below 60 degrees due to the presence of an underground furnace and to walls that were a massive three feet thick. Addison Baker Cresswell also built a stable block, completed in 1829, and filled the garden with a great variety of trees and shrubs.

Fig. 64 *Cresswell Hall, Northumberland, staircase (RCHME © Capt. A. J. Baker-Cresswell)*

He died in 1879 and was succeeded by his grandson Oswin and subsequently his great-grandson Addison Francis, who died in 1921. Three years later much of the estate was sold. The Hall was left unoccupied and at one stage the County Council considered using it for the mentally handicapped, but, due to the high costs of conversion and the possibility of subsidence, this plan was abandoned. The mansion consequently passed to the Ashington Coal Company and was occupied in 1932 by Thomas Boutland, the Traffic Manager, although already partially demolished. Flooring and other timber from the interior was offered for sale in 1934 and the house finally demolished in 1938.

Fig. 65 *Cresswell Hall, Northumberland, south front*   *(RCHME © Capt. A. J. Baker-Cresswell)*

Fig. 66 *Cresswell Hall, Northumberland, showing colonnade*

DILSTON CASTLE

The story of Dilston Castle and its owners is a romantic if tragic tale of devotion to the Church of Rome and the House of Stuart. The estate passed to the Radcliffe family via the marriage of the heiress Anne Cartington with Sir Edward Radcliffe, younger son of Thomas Radcliffe of Derwentwater in Cumberland. The family suffered intermittently under both the Tudors and the earlier Stuarts, being imprisoned for recusancy and accused of complicity in both the Gunpowder and the Popish plots.

The Castle was originally an L-shaped tower-house dating from the 15th century, but in about 1622 Sir Francis Radcliffe decided to enlarge it, incorporating the tower in a manor house (see fig.67) with mullioned and transomed windows, together with a chapel which survives today.

In 1709, James Radcliffe, Earl of Derwentwater, returned to Dilston, having been brought up at St. Germain's, in the company of the son of the exiled James II. Almost immediately he set about extending the mansion in a plain, almost barrack-like style (fig.68). The 'Fifteen', however, precipitately ended the main Radcliffe line. The Earl was executed for his part in the Rebellion, his son died a minor and the estates passed to the Greenwich Hospital Trust, who demolished the house in 1765 after it fell into disrepair. Dilston Hall was constructed on a different site in 1833 for the agriculturalist John Grey, agent for the Greenwich estates (see p.53).

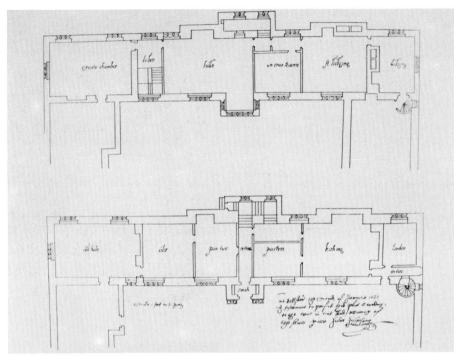

Fig. 67 *Plan for Dilston, Northumberland, by John Johnson, 1621*   *(NCH, x, p.290)*

Fig. 68 *Dilston Old Hall, Northumberland*   *(Mr. Jim Davidson)*

EARSDON WHITE HOUSE

This was the residence of the Barkers, prominent hereabouts since the 16th century. Christopher Barker (1732-71) was an attorney in Newcastle. The family changed its name to Purvis as a result of inheriting certain estates during the late 18th century, when the house was re-faced. However it was at least a century older and its garden had contained a small fortified tower. Used during the First World War as an Officers' Mess and later as a Working Men's Club, the house was purchased by Tynemouth Council in 1933 and demolished in 1959.

Fig. 69 *Earsdon White House, Northumberland* *(Northumberland County Council)*

ESHOTT HALL

Eshott is now two houses instead of one, the central block (see fig.70) having been demolished in the 1960s. William Carr (d.1674) is thought to have commissioned the eclectic mason-architect Robert Trollope, who rebuilt the Newcastle Guildhall from 1655, to build the original house. The Carrs added to the house during the 18th century but sold it in 1792 to Thomas Adams for £34,000. It later passed to the Brewis family of Swarland, who made extensive additions c.1850 including Rococo-style plaster work, executed by the Italians brought over to beautify Alnwick Castle. Eshott was purchased in 1887 by Emmerson Bainbridge of the Newcastle department store, who added an Italianate tower, and from the 1920s it was owned by the Sanderson family.

Fig. 70 *Eshott Hall, near Felton*
(Mr. P. R. B. Brooks)

FELTON PARK

Felton was originally held by the Lisle family, but passed to the Widdringtons via the marriage of the widow Dorothy Lisle to Edward Widdrington in 1661. Dorothy had been born Dorothy Horsley, daughter and co-heiress of Sir Thomas Horsley of Longhorsley, which led to her descendants becoming known as the Horsley Widdringtons and possessing not only Felton but also land at Longhorsley and Scrainwood.

Her grandson, Edward Horsley Widdrington, commissioned Felton Park to be built in 1732, to the designs of an architect named as Canston by Hodgson. The original house was two storeys in height over a half basement and is reminiscent of James Gibbs, with its heavy triple keystones over each window and quoins detailing the angles of the building. A heavy parapet and hipped roof surmounted the house, giving it a plain, solid appearance, typical of the earlier 18th century (see fig.72).

Edward Horsley Widdrington died in 1762, leaving his daughter Elizabeth as sole heir. The Horsley Widdringtons were Roman Catholics and probably as a consequence Elizabeth had married into another prominent Roman Catholic family, taking Thomas Riddell of Swinburne Castle as her husband in 1760, thus uniting the Swinburne and Felton estates.

Swinburne Castle was destined to be left to Thomas Riddell, the eldest son of the marriage, and Felton Park to Edward Horsley Widdrington Riddell, the second son; however, both sons died childless soon after inheriting and both estates passed to their younger brother Ralph, born in 1770. He added a plain east wing to the house at Felton, two storeys in

Fig. 71 *Felton Park, Northumberland*   *(Mr. Jim Davidson)*

Fig. 72 *Felton Park, Northumberland, main block*   *(Newcastle City Libraries and Arts)*

height and seven bays wide, with a datestone bearing his initials and the year 1799. This wing still survives, although the main house, which remained in the family until the 20th century, was demolished in 1952.

The success of the Riddell family in retaining their estates and acquiring new ones via marriage is notable. During the 18th and 19th centuries, the Riddells held the Swinburne, Felton and Cheeseburn Grange estates, and commissioned new mansions on all of them. Their success illustrates the ease with which Roman Catholics were assimilated into the Northumbrian elite even after the disastrous 1715 Rising. Despite being forced to register their estates, there were many Catholic families such as the Selbys of Biddlestone (see p.37), the Haggerstons of Haggerston (see pp.48-50), the Claverings of Callaly, and the Charltons of Hesleyside, who survived the political tides and found both the wherewithal and the inclination for architecture.

Fig. 73 *Felton Park, Northumberland, upper landing* (RCHME © Crown copyright)

HAGGERSTON CASTLE

The grounds of Haggerston Castle survive and are now a caravan park, an incongruous setting for Norman Shaw's Water Tower and Rotunda of 1893 which remain forlornly, the only indications of a palatial mansion which was swept away in 1931 after spiralling costs made it an impossible burden.

The Haggerston family were recorded as in possession of lands at Haggerston from the 12th century onwards. They persisted in their adherence to the Church of Rome, weathering the political and social storms of the 17th and 18th centuries, improving and expanding their estates, marrying well and adding to their capital.

The topographer Wallis recorded in 1769 that the family's seat was the old tower, kept in good repair, with the family arms on the south front. However, soon after this and prior to his death in 1777, Sir Thomas Haggerston constructed a new house of a very plain design, two storeys in height and seven bays wide with a pediment over the central salient and a semi-circular hood-moulding over the central first floor window. It is possible that Sir Thomas acted as his own architect, for his uncle had observed that "his great inclination of all is designing either in regard to these lovely or agreeable sciences, Architecture, Painting or Fortification".

Sir Thomas was succeeded by his son Carnaby, who in 1808 decided to expand the new house, adding three-storey wings of three bays either side of the central block. A note in his pocket-book names Luke Moody as the builder, and possibly the architect, since his fee was £1,787. Building continued until 1811 with the

Fig. 74 *Haggerston Castle, Northumberland, south elevation c.1905*

Fig. 75 *Haggerston Castle, Northumberland, Great Hall, as restored by J. B. Dunn   (from "The Builder", 23 July 1915)*

addition of domestic offices and servants' quarters.

Sir Carnaby died childless, his estates passing to his nephew, who bequeathed Haggerston to his great-nephew John Massey Stanley, an inveterate gambler who was forced to sell the estate to cover massive debts. Haggerston was thus sold in 1858 for £340,000 to John Naylor of Leighton Hall in Welshpool, who was the nephew of an entrepreneur who had amassed a fortune through shipping and banking interests. In 1889 John Naylor was succeeded by his son Christopher John, who adopted the additional name of Leyland to comply with his great uncle's will and set about improving his estate with ferocious energy.

It was at this point that Haggerston began to assume its gargantuan proportions, mushrooming from substantial Georgian house to Victorian white elephant. Leyland commissioned Norman Shaw to aggrandise the house between 1893 and 1897, much in the same way that the architect had previously enlarged Chesters. Shaw retained the old house, re-constructing the main reception rooms behind the original facade (see fig.74). In addition, he added three new wings around an internal courtyard, more than doubling the size of the house. Within this courtyard, Shaw designed a Great Hall of 84' x 40' (fig.75) entered from a monumental rotunda vestibule in the north-west corner. The whole design was further enhanced by a 153' water tower which provided storage space for three huge water tanks fed from the lake and a nearby spring, combining architectural drama and domestic practicality in a typically inventive Victorian manner.

Building continued into the 20th century with the construction of a new

Fig. 76 *Haggerston Castle, Northumberland, from the air* *(RCHME © Mrs. G. L. Y. Radcliffe)*

Fig. 77 *Haggerston Castle, Northumberland, south front as remodelled by J. B. Dunn*
(RCHME © Mrs. G. L. Y. Radcliffe)

stable block which, in addition to extensive stabling, also provided garage space for ten motor vehicles, servants' quarters and a staff ballroom used for Saturday evening dances. But fire ravaged Haggerston in 1911, destroying the central core of the house. Little daunted, Leyland set about rebuilding almost immediately, employing the Edinburgh architect James Dunn. The entire south and west elevations were redesigned (see figs.76 and 77), a new porte-cochère added and the rotunda extensively repaired.

The resulting 154-room mansion was inhabited for less than 20 years. C. J. Leyland died in 1923, leaving a vast mansion hampered by death duties, land taxes and rising costs. His son, Christopher Digby, sold off parts of the estate including the shooting-lodge Kidlandlee (see p.52) in an effort to raise funds, and lived in only a portion of the house. However, in 1930 the remaining 1,750 acres and the house went under the hammer. The only buyer who could be found was Mr. R. Dagnall of Cheshire, who organised the Castle's demolition and the auction of 2,247 lots including staircases, flooring, panelling and fireplaces, the last remnants of an architectural epic.

Fig. 78 *Haggerston Castle, Northumberland, dining room*   *(RCHME © Mrs. G.L.Y. Radcliffe)*

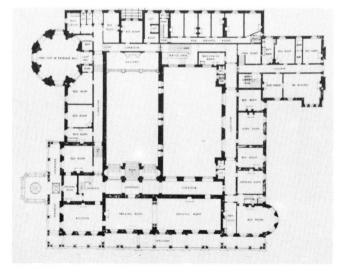

Fig. 79 *Haggerston Castle, Northumberland, plan of first floor   (from "The Builder", 23 July 1915)*

HEPPLE WOODSIDE

Hepple, west of Rothbury, contains a 14th-century ruined tower; an extensive mansion added to this does not survive. In the early 19th century the township was purchased from the Duke of Portland by Sir J. B. Riddell. This mid-Victorian mansion was on the left hand side of the B6341 going south-west, near the still-existing Hepple Whitefield. It was the property of Sir Walter B. Riddell and of his widow, Lady Alicia Riddell (c.1858-97) and later of Edward Newton (c.1897-1929). It was demolished c.1970. It was described, perhaps a little ungenerously, as "a comfortable stone house of no particular architectural distinction" (NCH, xv, p.381).

Fig. 80 *Hepple Woodside, near Rothbury*
(Mr. Jim Davidson)

HIRST CASTLE

This fortified farmhouse is included to give a flavour of the considerable quantity of Northumbrian vernacular architecture which has been destroyed. In Elizabethan times it is recorded as being in the possession of the Ogle family, from whom it passed to the Erringtons in the 18th century. The 'castle' stood in what are now the eastern suburbs of Ashington on the north side of Woodhorn Road, at that time a charming country lane. Hirst was demolished in 1908 for road-widening and residential development.

Fig. 81 *Hirst Castle, near Ashington*
(Mr. Jim Davidson)

HOLLYMOUNT HALL, BEDLINGTON

Situated at the end of what is now Hollymount Road, Hollymount was demolished c.1958 for residential development. It was built in 1844 by John Birkenshaw, Chief Agent of the Bedlington Iron Works and associate of George Stephenson and other railway pioneers. He sold the house about six years later to another iron-master, Michael Longridge (1785-1858), who had become Manager of the Works at the age of 24. Longridge greatly expanded the business, developing trade with the Blyth shipyards and exporting large quantities of iron to London via Blyth. He was also associated with George Stephenson, managing his locomotive works at Forth Banks, Newcastle.

Fig. 82 *Hollymount Hall, Bedlington*   *(Northumberland County Council)*

KIDLANDLEE MANSION

In a remote position on the moors north of Alwinton, in the foothills of the Cheviots, Kidlandlee had the distinction of being the highest 'mansion' in England at nearly 1,300 feet. It was built in the early 1890s by C. J. Leyland of Haggerston (see pp.48-50), on land purchased from the Hon. F. W. Lambton, as a shooting-box. In 1925 it was sold to the Lee family. By the late 1950s it had outlived its usefulness and was pulled down. Some cottages and the stable block remain.

Fig. 83 *Kidlandlee Mansion, near Alwinton*   *(Mr. P. R. B. Brooks)*

KILLINGWORTH HOUSE

This gigantic house stood on the south side of the village until 1954. The estate was purchased in 1737 by John Williams, who had built up considerable iron and glass interests. He died in 1763 and his son, another John, sold the house for 8,000 guineas four years later to the wholesale grocer George Colpitts. Tradition ascribes the design to Lancelot Coxon, who also worked at Roddam Hall, Northumberland, in the 1760s. William Newton made alterations during the 1770s, possibly the addition of the wings.

Towards the end of the century, the Colpitts were sharing the house with the Harrisons and the Reays. Later owners were John Jameson (from 1876) the McIntyres (c.1900-11) and the chemist Henry Eagle (from 1924).

Fig. 84 *Killingworth House, Northumberland* *(RCHME © Crown copyright)*

MILFIELD HILL

This early Victorian mansion, built on the site of an earlier house, was occupied by RAF personnel during the Second World War and demolished c.1967. The estate had been laid out by George Grey (d.1793) with help from the Culleys of Fowberry and his young son John (see p.44). John's daughter, Josephine Butler, recorded how her grandfather had first tackled the rugged country around Milfield "like a backwood settler", with an axe (NCH, xi, p.246).

Fig. 85 *Milfield Hill, near Wooler* *(Northumberland County Record Office)*

MITFORD OLD HALL

Mitford encapsulates the development of Northumbrian architecture with its castle, manor house and late Georgian villa. The Mitfords have long been associated with the village and left only recently when Mitford Hall (by Dobson, 1828) was sold. The castle was captured by William the Lion of Scotland in 1175. The manor house was probably constructed for Cuthbert Mitford, who died c.1593. The east front was remodelled in 1637, with a central porch tower, for Robert Mitford. Hodgson observed in 1832 that the greater part of the manor house had been demolished about twenty years earlier.

Fig. 86 *Mitford Old Hall, Northumberland* *(Newcastle City Libraries and Arts)*

NEWBIGGIN HALL (HOUSE), WESTERHOPE

During the 1960s the area became a major housing estate. Newbiggin Hall, off Newbiggin Lane, was built in the early 19th century, replacing an earlier house of the Hudson family (see p.65). In 1828 it was the residence of Henry, son of Matthew Bell M.P., of Woolsington, who had purchased the estate. Later residents were Lt.-Col. Charles James Reed, a brewer (c.1858-87), John Watson Spencer of Spencer's Steelworks, Newburn (from c.1887), and, from 1909, Gerald France M.P. He died in 1935 and his wife Hilda (née Bainbridge) in 1954. In the late 1950s, the Hall was replaced with a public house; this in turn has now been destroyed.

Fig. 87 *Newbiggin Hall, Westerhope* *(West Newcastle Local Studies)*

NEWBURN HALL

Newburn and Lemington industrialised early. Between the two villages was Lemington Hall, built in 1786 and demolished in 1953; it was the seat of Joseph Lamb, partner in the Northumberland Glass Company at Lemington. Here were also Bulmer's Iron Works. Newburn Hall, at the eastern end of the village near the river, consisted of a 15th-century pele tower to which a dwelling-house had been added c.1600. In 1765 Mrs. Lydia Bell, a widow, was living there. A later resident was Mrs. Elizabeth Hall (1855). In the early 19th century the property was still very extensive (see fig.88) but in 1891 the east wing burnt down. At about this time the Hall became incorporated into the former Spencer's Steel Works. Before the clearance of the site in the 1920s, it was used as a store for the pattern-shop.

Fig. 88 *Newburn Hall, Northumberland, c.1800*   *(Mr. P. R. B. Brooks)*

NEWBURN MANOR

This picturesque house of c.1600, with typical arched doorway and mullioned windows, was demolished in 1909. It stood half a mile west of the Hall, even closer to the river and again just north of the railway line. Fig.89 shows it from the south-west. Two fireplaces from the Manor are said to have been reinstated at Washington Old Hall. Its recorded residents included Thomas Finney, a surgeon, in the 1850s, and Thomas Hayes (in 1879).

Fig. 89 *Newburn Manor, Northumberland*   *(Newcastle City Libraries and Arts)*

NORTH SEATON HALL

It is often stated that John Dobson designed this fine classical house in 1813. However, the style is much earlier and it was noted by the Rev. John Horsley in 1730 that: "Mr. Watson built a good house here not long ago". This appears to corroborate the date of 1710 given in many directories. North Seaton also appears on Armstrong's Map of 1769. Dobson may have carried out alterations to the house in 1813. However, in 1831 he was definitely responsible for some buildings on the estate, including some workers' cottages and possibly the tower-like Gothic lodge (fig.91), although this is not in his usual style. North Seaton was situated in a wooded estate north of the present B1334 road to Ashington and was the seat of the Watson family until the late Victorian period. William Watson (d.1830) and his son, also William (b. c.1811), lived there for most of the first half of the 19th century and were noted for keeping a fine pack of hounds. By 1877, the Hall was occupied by Robert Watson and, by 1887, by the the industrialist Sir Isaac Lothian Bell, Lord Mayor of Newcastle and M.P. It was later owned by William Milburn and occupied by Mr. Charles Green and then by E. O. Southern. In the 1950s Pevsner found North Seaton "very neglected" and within a few years it had been pulled down.

Fig. 90 *North Seaton Hall, Northumberland* *(Northumberland County Council)*

Fig. 91 *North Seaton Hall, Northumberland, the lodge*
(Northumberland County Council)

ORDE HOUSE, MORPETH

This fine brick house originally consisted of several dwellings, the largest facing south, with a separate extension to the east and another house at right angles facing west. Demolished in 1967, it exemplified the kind of Georgian architecture which was considered expendable even in a historic market town and at this relatively recent date. A filling-station now occupies the site, on the southern approach to the town between the river and the former Courthouse (part of Dobson's County Gaol complex of 1822-28, built to replace the House of Correction standing behind Orde House). It was for the Governor of this earlier establishment, a Mr. Orde, that the house, or at least its largest component, was built in 1715.

Fig. 92 *Orde House, Morpeth (Mr. P. R. B. Brooks)*

OTTERBURN DENE HOUSE

Evidently Georgian with Victorian additions, Otterburn Dene was situated in extensive grounds by the Otter Burn, towards Hopedene — an area now incorporated into an army camp. In 1855 it was the residence of R. S. Coward, from c.1858 of Nicholas Wright, and from c.1887 of Richard Burdon-Sanderson. Major H. C. H. Hudson occupied it during the 1920s. Much of its estate was sold off in 1919 and the house demolished c.1970.

Fig. 93 *Otterburn Dene House   (Newcastle City Libraries and Arts)*

PAWSTON HALL

This was the residence of the ancient Selby family (see also pp.37, 65 and 69) who were related both to the Bigges and to William Clark (see pp.9 and 10). Its core was a fragmentary 16th-century pele tower. The house was greatly enlarged c.1870 and had also been rebuilt in the early 18th century. It is now a roofless ruin, although set, rather curiously, in well-tended gardens. Henry Collingwood Selby (1749-1839) bought the house from impecunious relatives in 1789; his only daughter died without issue, but his family, including Beauchamp Prideaux Selby (1841-1918), occupied the Hall until 1921, when it was sold to E. E. P. Taylor of Cornhill.

Fig. 94 *Pawston Hall, near Coldstream* *(Mr. Jim Davidson)*

RAY HOUSE

This Victorian house occupied a remote position overlooking the moors between Kirkwhelpington and West Woodburn, west of the A696. Built around three sides of a courtyard, it was popular with shooting parties and in the 1880s was occupied for this purpose by Henry T. Morton of Twizell House. Its most famous resident, from c.1910 until his death in 1931, was the famous engineer (and enthusiastic fisherman) Sir Charles Parsons, inventor of the steam turbine. A converted stable block, some cottages and a gamekeeper's lodge survive from the original estate.

Fig. 95 *Ray House, near Kirkwhelpington* *(Mr. Jim Davidson)*

SEATON LODGE

Situated near Seaton Sluice, this house was demolished early in the present century. Sir Ralph Delaval (d.1691) built up the Sluice as a port for the export of his salt, coal and stone. His son, Sir John, sold most of his property in 1719 to Admiral George Delaval, builder of Seaton Delaval Hall; on the site of this had been the manor house which Sir Ralph quit in 1685, under the terms of his son's marriage settlement, for Seaton Lodge. The Lodge is first mentioned in 1670, when in the possession of Thomas Harwood, master-mariner (NCH, ix, p.162). In the 1820s it was the residence of John Jobling, a coal-owner, and in 1900 of James Nelson.

Fig. 96 *Seaton Lodge, Seaton Sluice* (*Mr. Jim Davidson*)

SPARROW HALL, CULLERCOATS

Cullercoats was a fishing village containing also "respectable accommodation for visitors in the bathing season" (Pigot's *Directory*, 1834). As early as the 17th century the Doves were coal-owners in the area. Sparrow Hall (fig.97) was built in 1682 by Thomas Dove, son of John (and sold to a relative, Zepheniah Haddock, in 1706); a finial surmounting the east gable was carved with the initials of Thomas and Elizabeth Dove, together with the figure of a dove, hence the name "Sparrow Hall".

Fig. 97 *Sparrow Hall, Cullercoats* (*North Tyneside Central Library*)

SWARLAND PARK

Swarland Park is one of the few Northumbrian country houses with an identifiable architect, in this case almost certainly John Carr of York (1723-1807). Carr's only other known work in Northumberland is Chesters of 1771, later dramatically extended by Norman Shaw.

The Swarland estate was purchased in 1753 by Richard Grieve, a prosperous Alnwick solicitor. His son Davidson Richard Grieve, born in 1724, inherited it in 1765 and at once set about rebuilding. Davidson Grieve's trustees sold the estate in 1793 to Alexander Davison, who, in tribute to Nelson, planted the park to represent the position of the fleets at the Battle of the Nile. The Davison family continued to live at Swarland until the middle of the 19th century; it then passed through a variety of owners before being purchased by the Woods family of Benton Hall (see p.9), who held the house until 1922 when it was put up for auction.

It was purchased by the owners of Shilbottle, Longframlington and Whitton collieries to provide accommodation for miners, who evidently kept pigs in some of the bedrooms. In 1934, the Fountains Abbey Settlers Society purchased the estate and laid out nearly 80 houses in the park with streets named, appropriately, Nelson Drive, Park Road and The Avenue. The mansion was reported as being in the hands of house-breakers in the same year.

Fig. 98 *Swarland Park, Northumberland*   *(Mr. P. R. B. Brooks)*

Fig. 99 *Swarland Park, Northumberland, interior*   *(RCHME © Crown copyright)*

SWINBURNE CASTLE

The Swinburne estate was sold in 1678 by William, third Lord Widdrington, to Thomas Riddell of Fenham, son of Sir Thomas Riddell, a former governor of Tynemouth Castle who had supported the Royalists during the Civil War and was therefore exiled abroad until his death in 1652. His son attended the English College in Rome and became a Roman Catholic. Much is made of the decline of the Northumbrian Catholic families who were pushed aside in the 18th century, but the Riddells were a Catholic success story as already evidenced at Felton Park (see pp.46-47).

Thomas Riddell died in 1704 leaving his estates to his son Edward, who, under the requirements of the penal laws, registered them in 1717. He was evidently a man of wealth, his income augmented by collieries still retained near Fenham. His son Thomas married Mary, heiress to the Cheeseburn Grange estate, in 1726, and commissioned the building of new stables at Swinburne marked "TMR1728" and emblazoned with a fine coat of arms. Their son, another Thomas, succeeded in 1754 and married Elizabeth Horsley Widdrington, heiress of the Felton Park estate. The Cheeseburn estate went to their second surviving son Ralph. Thomas decided to demolish the old castle at Swinburne and rebuild, possibly to his own design. Wallis observed in 1769 that the new house was "of his own erection out of the ruins of the old castle after a very neat design". Thomas built the 5-bay central block first, adding the 3-bay canted wings in 1771 (fig.100). The new castle had some fine plaster ceilings in the Adam style (figs.101 and 102). A further new stable block and an elegant orangery

Fig. 100 *Swinburne Castle, Great Swinburne, from the south-west* *(RCHME © Crown copyright)*

Fig. 101 *Swinburne Castle, Great Swinburne, room in south wing* *(RCHME © Crown copyright)*

61

were also added about this time. The Castle was demolished c.1966, but both the stable blocks survive as does the small Roman Catholic chapel, designed in 1841.

Fig. 102 *Swinburne Castle, Great Swinburne, detail of ceiling of room in south wing (RCHME © Crown copyright)*

TILLMOUTH PARK

Both Tillmouth Park and Twizell Castle were the creations of the Blake family, who also remodelled Fowberry Tower, near Wooler, in 1776. Clearly inspired by the Gothic Revival, four generations built, altered, demolished, and rebuilt following the fashions of the time. Tillmouth was purchased by Sir Francis Blake I (second creation) about 1740 and, after the sale of Fowberry in 1807, became the principal family residence, despite being only a short distance from Twizell Castle. Probably rebuilt (fig.103) around 1810 by Sir Francis Blake II, it was demolished in the 1880s by his grandson to create the house that survives on a different site as a hotel, surrounded by the gardens of the earlier house.

Fig. 103 *Tillmouth Park, from the north-west* (RCHME © Crown copyright)

TWIZELL CASTLE

Originally owned by the Selby family, a branch of which settled at Twizell House (p.65), the Twizell estate near Wooler was sold to Sir Francis Blake in 1685 for a little less than £2,000. Its story is perhaps the most long-running saga in Northumberland's architectural history. The topographer Wallis observed in 1769 that the Castle had been "lately repaired with handsome additions chiefly in the Saxon Gothic style" — presumably by Sir Francis Blake I (second creation).

These early alterations and additions failed to satisfy the second Sir Francis, who succeeded his father in 1780, as work continued throughout the decade and was observed with interest by Blake's neighbour, Col. Horace St. Paul. St. Paul was improving nearby Ewart Park in a similar castellated style and indeed was the recipient of various unwanted architectural items from Twizell, including, legend has it, an entire tower. Sir Francis Blake's cousin, Sir John Hussey Delaval, was also a keen Goth, altering Ford Castle from 1765, and it is thought that they shared the services of the mason-architect James Nesbit of Kelso.

Twizell Castle fits snugly into the early Gothic Revivalism described in the Introduction, looking as if it was constructed from gingerbread and icing rather than stone and mortar. Building at the Castle continued for a further half-century, causing the topographer Raine to acidly comment in 1852 that instead of the old pele tower there now stood "an unseemly mass of unfinished masonry... possessing no one single feature of castellated architecture save that it is in the shape of a parallelogram, with wide pointed mullionless windows and a huge

Fig. 104 *Twizell Castle, Northumberland, detail*
(RCHME © Sir Michael Blake)

disproportionate round bastion at each corner". This statement aptly illustrates the mid-Victorian Goth's horror of the frivolous structures of preceding generations, lacking as they were in archaeological exactitude.

Sir Francis is thought to have expended £80,000 on Twizell in addition to his works at Tillmouth Park (p.62). Reduced now from its original five storeys to a moss- and ivy-clad ruin, there is little to suggest Twizell's former glory as the embodiment of an 18th-century conception of a medieval castle. Perhaps, as Raine said, this ruin is a "melancholy memorial of the most extreme want of taste" or perhaps, put more kindly, it represents an almost endearing, boundless enthusiasm for Gothic architecture.

Fig. 105 *Twizell Castle, Northumberland* *(RCHME © Sir Michael Blake)*

Fig. 106 *Twizell Castle, Northumberland, from the river* *(RCHME © Sir Michael Blake)*

TWIZELL HOUSE

George Selby purchased Twizell House and its estate of 643 acres in 1790. It is likely that the house was already built by this date, as stylistically it is essentially Palladian. The Ionic portico was a later addition by George Wyatt for Prideaux John Selby, the son of the purchaser, in 1812. P. J. Selby had succeeded to the estate in 1798 and became a notable ornithologist, known for his fine illustrations. He also published *British Forest Trees*, based on his planting schemes at Twizell. Fig.107 shows the crisp, clean lines of the house, which was demolished c.1960, obscured by a later sun room.

Fig. 107 *Twizell House, near Adderstone   (RCHME © Crown copyright)*

WHITLEY HALL

The Hudsons had coal mines in Whitley from the late 17th century. Henry Hudson (1720-89) built this house in about 1760 (adding the wings in 1776), replacing his earlier seat. His widow bequeathed it in 1815 to her niece Hannah Ellison, from whom it was purchased by the Duke of Northumberland. Later it was the residence of J. H. Friar (d.1855), Mrs. Lydia Green, and then of M. W. Lambert (c.1873-93). Ultimately the small estate was offered to the Council as a park, but refused, and the Hall, on a site now occupied by the police station in Laburnum Avenue, was demolished in 1899.

Fig. 108 *Whitley Hall, Whitley Bay   (North Tyneside Central Library)*

WHITLEY PARK

Whitley was described in 1834 as "a very respectable and neat little village close to the sea". Its population was at that time 632. Edward Hall of Flatworth, breeder of the fat ox immortalised in one of Bewick's engravings, built Whitley Park in about 1789 (the right hand portion as seen in fig.109 seems to have been a later addition). The house was covered with white stucco. After Mr. Hall's death in 1792, the Park was sold to John Haigh, a 'hostman'. In 1800 it was purchased by Thomas Wright of North Shields and in 1844 sold to J. H. Hinde. Later residents included Thomas Davison (in 1845), C. M. Palmer (in 1855) and T. W. Bulman (1869-79), whose widow occupied it until c.1891. After further changes of ownership, it became the Park Hotel in 1897, with most of the land being sold off for building purposes. In 1922 Whitley Park was bought for use as Council offices but was demolished (see fig.110) in 1939. A library and a small park (with some mature trees) now occupy the site of what was left of its estate.

Fig. 109 *Whitley Park, Whitley Bay*   *(North Tyneside Central Library)*

Fig. 110 *Whitley Park, Whitley Bay, under demolition*   *(North Tyneside Central Library)*

WIDDRINGTON CASTLE

In 1832 this was described as ancient and "now obliterated" (Hodgson). Licence to crenellate had been granted in 1341 and the old tower clearly resembled that at Belsay. The bay window and decorative finials were later additions.

The Widdringtons were attainted for their part in the Rebellion of 1715 and their estates passed in 1761 to Sir George Warren. He pulled down the original castle. Legend had it that upon asking the advice of a friend about a new design, he was handed the Buck engraving (fig.111). The castle was rebuilt but destroyed by fire. Undaunted, Sir George tried once more, constructing a "slight fantastical building possessing neither grandeur nor convenience" by Thomas Sewell of Alnwick some time after 1778. Octagonal in shape, this had Venetian windows on the ground floor and quatrefoil windows lighting the upper rooms, being last occupied in 1802.

Fig. 111 *Widdrington Castle, Northumberland, by S. and N. Bucks, 1728 (detail)*

WOODHORN MANOR

Woodhorn Manor (fig.112) was demolished during the 1970s. Sir Jacob Wilson, Director of the Royal Agricultural Society, lived there in the 1870s, as did James Edwards in 1887, and Robert Gray, a farmer, between 1897 and 1929. Near it was also Woodhorn Demesne, occupied by A. J. Baker Cresswell while building Cresswell Hall (see pp.41-43) and removed c.1965.

Fig. 112 *Woodhorn Manor, Northumberland* (Beamish, North of England Open Air Museum)

MORE LOST HOUSES OF NORTHUMBERLAND

Of the county's lost houses not already mentioned a substantial proportion were to be found in the increasingly developed area immediately north and east of Newcastle, towards the coast. Thus, for example, in Monkseaton, were two houses of rather greater importance than their names suggest, **Rock Cottage** and **Burnt House Farm**, demolished in 1965 and c.1929 respectively. The former was situated at the Chapel Lane end of Bygate Road and, although older, bore a date plaque of 1821. The latter, at the top of Bromley Avenue, was the property of John Reay (d.1715). The former "Ship Inn" in Front Street, Monkseaton, was originally a house built by Thomas Mills in 1688 containing an elaborate stucco frieze with the arms of Charles II. It became an inn about 1790 and was demolished in the 1920s, the present public house being built near the site.

Whitley House was a large brick residence standing near the present Coliseum Cinema and Victoria Hotel in Whitley Road, Whitley Bay. Owned by the Hudsons and then the Halls, it was purchased in 1803 by Thomas Stephens, who appears to have partially rebuilt it. Later occupants included members of the Ilderton family, S. W. Parker, H. Mitcalfe, Mrs. Lydia Green, Henry Bell, and, in the late 19th century, Lawrence William Adamson. Not far away was **St. Paul's Vicarage**, on the site of a terrace of shops in Park View erected after its demolition in 1933. It was designed by Anthony Salvin in 1865.

Just off the present Linskill Terrace, North Shields, stood **Tynemouth Lodge**, a brick house of three storeys with projecting canted bays, built in 1790 by

Fig. 113 *Waterville House, North Shields*   *(North Tyneside Central Library)*

Colonel William Linskell. He was the first Mayor of Tynemouth and was still in residence in the 1820s, but the Lodge was demolished in 1858. Also in North Shields, a desirable village in the early 19th century, were **Campville**, north of Cleveland Road (built 1814 for the shipowner John Fenwick and demolished in the early 20th century), the adjacent **Cleveland House**, residence in the mid-19th century of R. D. Mease, a manufacturing chemist, and **West Chirton House**. The last-named was designed by Dobson in 1819 for Michael Robson, a coal-owner, who occupied it until at least 1834; John Hedley owned it in the late 19th century. It stood to the south-west of **Chirton House** (see p.39) on the site of the present West Chirton Trading Estate, and was demolished c.1937. Also by Dobson were **Hylton Lodge** (for Thomas Hughes, occupying

the site of the present St. Cuthbert's School, on the corner of Coach Lane and Lovaine Place), **Preston Villa** (1819, for John Fenwick, uncle of Fenwick of **Campville**), a stone-built classical house demolished in 1967 to make way for the "Woodlands" residential development, and **Waterville House**, designed in 1815 for R. Rippon and later occupied by George Rippon. This became incorporated into Stanley Street West (see fig.113) and was destroyed by bombing on 30th September 1941. **South Preston Lodge** dated from about 1800 and stood north of Albion Road near the present South Preston Grove. In the early 19th century it was the residence of Thomas Fenwick; its last known owner or tenant was Alfred Belcher in 1924. **Ingleside** was an Italianate villa built c.1878 for the shipowner Joseph Robinson, west of Preston Road on the site of the present Ingleside Road and Preston Park development. It was demolished shortly after the Second World War.

Further north was **Cramlington House**, built c.1815 by Adam Mansfeldt de Cardonnel Lawson after demolishing his old mansion at Chirton; he inherited both estates from the Lawson family. A plain classical design by Dobson, in the area of the present Lanercost Hall estate, East Cramlington, it was demolished c.1969. Another lost house was **Crow Hall**, about a mile north-west of Cramlington. In the early 19th century it was occupied as a boarding school by the Rev. W. D. Thompson, Curate of Horton. The demolition of **Bedlington Old Hall** (fig.114), in the early 1960s, was a blatant example of the indifference, even hostility, shown to historic buildings at this time. Consisting of a 15th-century pele with a substantial block added probably in the early 18th century, the Hall had become a workers' tenement after about 1846. It was replaced by some undistinguished council offices, referring to which a local councillor stated in 1959: "We propose to demolish the Old Hall and Keep which for centuries have dominated our Front Street ... we desire to use that very desirable site in a much better way".

Moving northwards along the Northumberland coast, there was **Bullock's Hall**, between Widdrington and Acklington, seat of a branch of the Mitford family, and **Mid Hall**, the early 17th-century residence of the Salkelds, demolished by the late 19th century. **Gloster Hill** was a late 17th-century manor house, owned by the Lawson family, a mile north-west of Amble. Descriptions suggest that it might have been by, or in the manner of, Trollope. the house declined in status during the 19th century and was

Fig. 114 *Bedlington Old Hall, Northumberland (RCHME © Crown copyright)*

demolished in the late 1930s. However, some fireplaces from it were incorporated into Dunstan Hall, near Craster, in 1939.

A particularly regrettable loss was **Swansfield House**, built by Dobson for Henry Collingwood Selby in 1823 on the south-west outskirts of Alnwick and demolished c.1975. Ironically, a neo-Georgian house was built on the site. A column commemorating the short-lived peace of Europe in 1814 still survives from the estate. Meanwhile, even in Berwick, a fine Georgian villa at no. **18 Blackwell Road** was not immune from destruction during the 1970s.

Comparatively few lost houses of the type discussed in this book existed elsewhere in Northumberland, but mention should be made of the following: **Birdhopecraig Hall**, off the A68 near Rochester; **Birtley Hall**, a ruined house of c.1611 built on to an earlier tower and owned by a branch of the Heron family; **Weldon Hall** near Brinkburn, home of the Lisles since at least the 17th century and

demolished in the 1890s; and **Woodhall**, near Holystone, a 17th-century house demolished in the late 1960s. **Blackhall Hill**, near Simonside, and **Mounces**, west of Bellingham, were shooting-boxes. The former was built c.1700 by Sir William Blackett but was burnt down by gypsies in 1812. The latter was owned by Sir John Swinburne of Capheaton during the early 19th century; it was submerged during the construction of the Kielder Reservoir.

More substantial was **Brandon White House**, built early in the 18th century by Lancelot Allgood, a Newcastle attorney, and enlarged sometime after 1739 by his son, also Lancelot. Situated on the A697 eight miles south of Wooler, it was burnt down after the Second World War. Also important was **Collingwood House**, the early 19th-century seat of John Collingwood Tarleton at Little Ryle, about five miles west of Whittingham. In 1848 it was bought by the Liddells of nearby Eslington House, but was allowed to decay and had disappeared by 1895.

BIBLIOGRAPHY
AND REFERENCES

H. A. Adamson, *Old Landmarks in the Parish of Tynemouth* (1898).

A. and J. Airey, *The Bainbridges of Newcastle, a Family History 1697-1976* (1979).

W. Andrews, *Bygone Northumberland* (1899).

W. Angus, *Seats of the Nobility and the Gentry* (1787).

C. E. Baldwin, *The History and Development of the Port of Blyth* (1929).

M. Barke and R. J. Buswell (eds), *Newcastle's Changing Map* (1992).

Benwell Community Project, *The Making of a Ruling Class* (1978).

R. Bibby, *Bothal Observed* (1973).

R. Bibby, *Borough of Morpeth Official Guide* (1966).

H. Bourne, *The History of Newcastle upon Tyne* (1736).

J. R. Boyle and W. H. Knowles, *Vestiges of Old Newcastle and Gateshead* (1890).

J. Brand, *The History and Antiquities of the Town and County of Newcastle upon Tyne* (1789).

P. Brown, *The Friday Books of North Country Sketches,* 4 vols (1934-46).

S. and N. Buck, *Views of Old Castles and Priories in the Counties of Northumberland and Durham* (edition of 1899, first published 1728).

J. B. Burke, *Visitation of Seats,* 2 vols (1852-53).

W. Burns, *Newcastle: a Study in Replanning at Newcastle upon Tyne* (1967).

J. Butler, *Memoir of John Grey of Dilston* (1874).

W. Campbell, *High Elswick 100 Years Ago* (1973).

E. Charlton, *Society in Northumberland in the Last Century* (1874).

A. H. Cochrane, *The Early History of Elswick* (1909).

H. M. Colvin, *A Biographical Dictionary of British Architects 1600-1840,* 3rd ed. (1995).

J. M. Crook, "Northumbrian Gothick", in *Journal of the Royal Society of Arts,* vol.cxxi (1973), pp.271-83.

W. Davison, *A Descriptive and Historical View of Alnwick* (1822).

F. W. Dendy, *An Account of Jesmond* (1904).

F. W. Dendy, *Three Lectures on Old Newcastle, its Suburbs, and Gilds, etc.* (1921).

D. D. Dixon, *Upper Coquetdale, Northumberland* (1903).

D. D. Dixon, *Whittingham Vale, Northumberland* (1895).

S. F. Dixon, *History of the Saxon Royal Town of Corbridge upon Tyne* (1912).

J. Dobson, *Plan of Estates and Premises the Property of William Clark Esq. Little Benton, Northumberland* (1813).

J. Donald, *Bygone Jesmond* (1987).

J. Donald, *Not Just Bricks and Mortar* (1994).

W. C. Donkin, *An Outline Bibliography of the Northern Region* (1956).

T. S. Earnshaw, *Hartley and Old Seaton Sluice: a Short History* (1957).

Elswick Local History Group, *Richardson's Leatherworks – the Workers' Story* (1985).

T. E. Faulkner, "Conservation and Renewal in Newcastle upon Tyne", in Faulkner (ed.), *Northumbrian Panorama* (1996), pp.123-48.

T. E. Faulkner, "The Early 19th Century Planning of Newcastle upon Tyne", in *Planning Perspectives,* v (1990), pp.149-67.

T. E. Faulkner and A. Greg, *John Dobson: Newcastle Architect, 1787-1865* (1987).

R. Forster, *History of Corbridge and its Antiquities* (1881).

J. Fuller, *The History of Berwick-upon-Tweed* (1799).

V. Gibbs et al (eds) *The Complete Peerage by G.E.C.,* 13 vols (1910-40).

W. S. Gibson, *Dilston Hall* (1850).

F. Graham, *The Old Halls, Houses and Inns of Northumberland* (1977).

W. Gray, *Chorographia, or a Survey of Newcastle* (1649).

F. Green et al, *A Guide to the Historic Parks and Gardens of Tyne and Wear* (1995).

J. Grundy, *Report on the Historic Buildings of the Northumberland National Park* (n.d.).

J. Hall, *A Guide to Wooler and Neighbourhood* (1895).

G. Harbottle, *Gosforth and its Parish Church* (n.d.).

W. P. Hedley, *Northumbrian Families,* 2 vols (1968).

J. Hodgson, *A History of Northumberland,* 7 vols (1820-58).

J. Hodgson, *Topographical and Historical Description of the County of Northumberland* (1817).

J. Hodgson, *The Picture of Newcastle* (1812).

M. Holmes, *The Country House Described* (1986).

J. Horsley, *Materials for the History of Northumberland* (1730).

E. Hughes, *North Country Life in the 18th Century: the North East, 1700-1750* (1952).

W. Hutchinson, *A View of the County of Northumberland,* 2 vols (1778).

C. E. Jackson, *Prideaux John Selby* (1992).

J. Jamieson, *Northumberland at the Opening of the 20th Century,* ed. by W. T. Pike (1905).

P. Lowery, "Patronage and the Country House in Northumberland", in T. E. Faulkner (ed.), *Northumbrian Panorama* (1996), pp.49-73.

P. Lowery, "William Newton — an Eminent Architect?", in T. E. Faulkner (ed.) "Northumbrian Heritage", special issue of *Northern Architect* (Winter 1994-95, 5th series, issue 1).

E. Mackenzie, *A Descriptive and Historical Account of the Town and County of Newcastle upon Tyne* (1827).

E. Mackenzie, *An Historical, Topographical and Descriptive View of the County of Northumberland* (1825).

G. Mark, *A Survey of a Portion of Northumberland* (1734).

A. Mawer, *The Place-names of Northumberland and Durham* (1920).

S. Middlebrook, *Newcastle upon Tyne, its Growth and Achievement* (1950).

J. Murray (publisher), *A Handbook for Travellers in Durham and Northumberland* (1864 and later editions).

Newbiggin Local History Group, *A History of Newbiggin Hall Estate 1960-1988* (1989).

Northumberland County History Committee,

History of Northumberland, 15 vols (1893-1940).
Northumberland County Record Office (Morpeth), Sale Catalogues of Northumbrian Houses: CLA Series.
Northumberland County Record Office, *The Making of the Northumberland Landscape*, ex.cat. (1974).
T. Oliver, *A New Picture of Newcastle upon Tyne* (1831).
L. Palmer, *Bygone Kenton* (1993).
N. Pevsner et al, *The Buildings of England: Northumberland* (1957 and 1992 editions).
T. Quinn, *Bygone Benwell* (1990).
T. Quinn, *Bygone Scotswood* (1991).
J. Raine, *The History and Antiquities of North Durham* (1852).
M. A. Richardson, *Descriptive Companion Through Newcastle upon Tyne and Gateshead* (1838).
W. Richardson, *History of the Parish of Wallsend* (1923).
A. Saint, *Richard Norman Shaw* (1976).
A. Scott, *Historical Guide to Rothbury and Surrounding District* (1885).
J. Slinn, *A Souvenir History of Haggerston Castle* (1995).
G. Tate, *The History of the Borough, Castle and Barony of Alnwick*, 2 vols (1866-69).
H. A. Taylor, *Northumberland History* (1963).
W. W. Tomlinson, *Comprehensive Guide to Northumberland* (1888 and later editions).
W. W. Tomlinson, *Historical Notes on Cullercoats, Whitley and Monkseaton* (1893).
W. W. Tomlinson, *The Village of Chirton and its Associations* (limited edition, 1891).
Tyne & Wear Archives, Dr. C. M. Brooks Archive on Longbenton: DBC Series.
J. Wallis, *The Natural History and Antiquities of Northumberland*, 2 vols (1769).
A. D. Walton, *Bygone Westgate Road* (1993).
A. D. Walton, "Sir William Stephenson" in *Wesley History Society North East Branch Bulletin,* nos 32 and 33 (1979-80).
W. Watts, *Seats of the Nobility and the Gentry* (1779-86).
R. Welford, *History of Newcastle and Gateshead*, 3 vols (1884-87).
R. Welford, *A History of the Parish of Gosforth* (1879).
R. Welford, *Men of Mark 'twixt Tyne and Tweed*, 3 vols (1895).
H. Whitaker, *A Descriptive List of the Maps of Northumberland, 1576-1900* (1949).
L. Wilkes and G. Dodds, *Tyneside Classical* (1964).
D. F. Wilson, *A Handbook to Morpeth and the Neighbourhood* (1876).
A. B. Wright, *An Essay Towards a History of Hexham* (1823).

INDEX OF HOUSES